At the Stein
shoulder-buddy
Belong. Bring y
jams. Bring conundrums and pesky syllogisms. Bring loves renewed or dreamed or left at the subway platform. Make note. Bring your hope-with-disillusion. Whether wizened or supple, the Stein servers-and-preservers, all sharpen the wort of Shaner's human moment like the bold hops for which Northwest ales are known. Our summers grow hotter. So have a gulp. Listen, and counter. Some drink to remember, Tim Shaner is one of *that* sum.

Tim Whitsel
author of *We Say Ourselves* and *Wishmeal*

In *Noch Ein at the Stein*, Tim Shaner captures the essential elements of why the Stein is my favorite bar in America. The beer community, the stories, the very human social contact & interaction, and, above all, the celebration of beer - I have experienced all these and more at "the Stein," even meeting a poet of note. *Noch Ein* is a must read for all those who love bar life and life itself. It is even more poignant during these Covid times when that sense of "Communitas" has been taken away.

Hal Hermanson
KLCC Brewfest Operations/Brewer's Lounge, Underwriting, & fellow

Noch Ein
at the Stein

*A poetic essay
on beer, conversation,
and hippycrits*

Tim Shaner

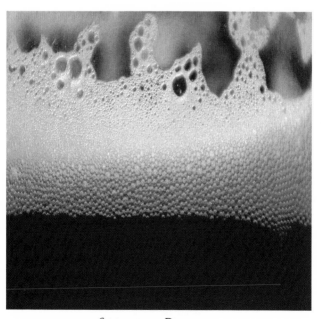

SPUYTEN DUYVIL

NEW YORK CITY

Thanks to Barbara Henning who, when in town to give a reading, encouraged me to write a book about Eugene, to my late friend Charlie Butcher (aka Bill Burroughs) for his unforgettable companionship, to my many interlocutors (friends), whose names have been changed to protect their innocence, and to the beer community in general for the spark of rejuvenation it ignited in this town before Covid closed things down. Lastly, gratitude and love to Tammy and Nora and her partner Ben, who designed such an amazing cover.

Library of Congress Cataloging-in-Publication Data

Names: Shaner, Tim, author.
Title: Noch ein at the stein : a poetic essay on beer, conversation, and hippycrits / Tim Shaner.
Description: New York City : Spuyten Duyvil, [2021] |
Identifiers: LCCN 2021039901 | ISBN 9781956005295 (paperback)
Subjects: LCGFT: Essays.
Classification: LCC PS3619.H35466 N63 2021 | DDC 814/.6--dc23
LC record available at https://lccn.loc.gov/2021039901

for Charlie Butcher

"…we are stuck in an imaginary impasse, living on while not knowing what to do…"

—Lauren Berlant

At the Stein again. Didn't feel like conversing this time, though. But yet to snuggle-up (dreaded-word) to my but yet book, in this case, *A Tonalist* by Laura Moriarty, anxious to figure out what all this *a tonalism* stuff is all about and whether I too could be an *a tonalist*. I've noticed that when I read these manifestos, whatever they are, I automatically want to be part of that group, to merge with the collective text—that's my nature. Or perhaps it's the nature of reading, wherein one's body becomes the text while in the act of reading it. Follow me? Putting it down and picking it up, till it's done, flipping page after page to the very last page, your hands, your fingers, your face in the book. Bill Burroughs was there. I could have sat next to him, given the empty seat at the bar next to him, but chose instead to sit at the end of the bar, my favorite spot. Besides, I wanted to read. Having just acquired six new books. When you first get books, it's like it is with cds, or records, back then in the day before vinyl became popular again. You just want to fondle the things, in their freshness, before they've been worn through, done in, familiarized, forgotten, remaindered, just more pile in the junk, though, with books, real books, it's a *library*, like your brain folded inside out, as someone recently said, that being how I saw New York City when I lived there, as humanity's brain, *folded inside out*

This has happened the last few times I've been at the Stein. Going there, with book in hand, knowing I'll probably end up talking to someone, at the bar, which is why I go there, but, unlike today, not reading my book—but yet it's all conversation one way and another

And it's all about being at the bar, isn't it, not just *in* the bar, at one of the tables—though a good table can make for a fine companion, if I may—but *at* the bar. Actually, in fact, there is one table at the Stein that is my go-to table when the bar's *all taken*. All the other tables at the Stein are at the level of the bar, with four bar stools/chairs per table, they planned it that way, deciding that they wanted everybody sitting at the same level, rather than having some at a lower level and some at a higher level, thereby avoiding a distinction, a divide, between those at the bar and those at the tables, as if those at the tables weren't drinking every bit as much as those at the bar. But with this table, my so-called go-to table, the only one of its kind there, this table in question is short and sits just two, standing alone, off to the side, almost invisible, down there amid the tall tables, apart, yet *in it*. I like sometimes to sit there alone, submerged, below the fray, and read my book, below everybody, mostly out of sight, below the chatter, the louder the chatter the easier to read. Had I the choice to sit at the bar, I would, of course, choose the bar instead of the table, since it's all about being at the bar, isn't it, not just in the bar but *at* the bar, even when I just want to go there and read, which may appear to be a privatized gesture but in fact reading is a public act, all conversation, one way and another

As for those who choose the tables instead of the bar, high or low, it's like they are saying to the others in the bar that they're not there to meet with them, with those who happen to wander in off the street, friend or stranger, who saunter up to the bar and take a seat, who risk a chance encounter and the conversation to come, but to meet with someone else from *the outside* as planned, just the two of you there at your table, as planned, meeting with some *outsider,* a date, or maybe three or four of you, you often see these sorts sitting there initially alone, at a table instead of the bar, in wait of a friend or a lover, who more than likely has no sense of loyalty to the place in question, who has no book in hand, it's like they are saying to the others in the bar, those at the bar as well as those at the adjacent tables, that they're not there to meet with those who come to the Stein regularly or fresh off the street for the first time, in order to chance upon an encounter, and through that build a family of sorts, or rather a family away from *the family*, a family of comings and goings, but to sit there alone, sans book, waiting for their friends, alone in their privatized space, curling in on their mobile device, most likely, hunched over it fondling the smart buttons and all, swishing this smart way and that, the fingers busy thumbing, or swishing instead, this way and that, curled in on oneself, waiting for their outsider, their table a privatized place, an individualized zone, roped off in effect

But because this is the Stein, the original Stein, when the Stein was small and cozy and ripe for conversation, eventually the Stein would get so packed that the separation between those who sat at the tables and those who sat at the bar would disappear, coming there alone, choosing a table over the bar or the bar over the table, at a certain point in the evening, several pints in, the distinction between those at the tables, tables at the same height as the bar, as planned, would disappear, thereby fusing together all and one, those at their formerly privatized or individualized tables rubbing up against those at the bar, becoming one big family of sorts, with everyone in good cheer, conversations merging, slopping over from the bar to the tables and from one table to the next, the conversations merging and slurring, breaking down the distinction between the private-minded drinkers and the public-minded drinkers

Sometimes I run into Jack Kerouac, to be distinguished from Jack Spicer, who works at the Stein. Jack's in charge of the kegs and bottles. There's also Jackson McLow, the other Jack who works behind the bar. We get along with all the Jacks in question, though sometimes, conversing at the Stein with one of the Steinians, I'd mention running into Jack at say The Highlands or the Lope, as in Jack-a-Lope, and there'd initially be some confusion about which Jack was the Jack in question, none of us knowing the others' last names, at first. The Stein was featured in the *New York Times* as an example of a new trend in pubs in the USA—those modeled, but in their own hoppy way, after wine bars, but only insofar as they treat beer with the sort of care wine traditionally has been treated, but why define it negatively, according to what it isn't? Needless to say, it is definitely not a wine bar, not that I don't like wine bars, me liking anything with bar in the name, but the Stein, according to the *Times*, was a new sensation, a rather unique combination of bar, restaurant, and beer store, what they now call a bottle shop, with some five hundred different beers, domestic and international, on their shelves, and some twenty taps constantly in rotation, featuring mostly local beer from the West Coast but also the rare German or Belgium brew, a Hefeweizen or ales made by Trappist monks, all of which were in constant rotation such that no one beer was regularly on tap. This time, however, it was Neal Cassidy at the Stein when I went there. I've come to realize, after speaking to Neal Cassidy, that telling people in Eugene I'm writing a book on Eugene opens the floodgates in terms of storytelling, the plan initially being to write a book about Eugene and its aging hippies, the new greatest generation, I would argue, the original "greatest generation" not really being that great, after all, but it eventually morphed into *Noch Ein at the Stein*, a book all about being at the Stein, at the bar preferably, though, to be fair, just to be *in* the Stein suffices in my book, being sometimes inclined to sit away from the bar in order to converse with my book, to be, in other words, anti-social but in a public setting, at first at least, until, a couple drafts in, I gravitate away from the book's conversation to the live version of face to face dialectics, a bar stool suddenly opening up, say. Not that I'm interested in stories, that is, stories with their narrative arc and all, triangulating toward some conclusion, some closure. Neal Cassidy had a load of stories to tell, however, and he told me two today. I told him when I left not to worry, I have a bad memory and won't take the stories he was feeding me and repeat them here in the alleged book on Eugene, as if I can remember them. Neal Cassidy, who's a total hipster, but of the older sort, not what they mean today by hipster, believes in reincarnation, I learned today. That's okay, I mean it's him believing that, not me. Though true he's reincarnated here in this book, as it were, for a stretch, at least, maybe. I tell him that for me life's just life, mysterious, yes, but familiarly so, familiarly an enigma, nothing to feel alienated about, to get all angsty about. Maybe I'll start thinking about death again when I'm closer to the end (not that it's not always close at hand or that it's not already right here now, *right now*, RIGHT NOW), but, considering how my parents are dealing with it, I'm not so sure about that. I get the sense from my parents that they decidedly *don't* want to talk about death, given that soon they'll both be knocking on heaven's door, sooner than later, more or less. So, maybe it's the other way around, that the closer you get to death, the less you want to think about it, much less talk about it, wanting to think life, instead, walking & talking it and *living* it, living it and remembering it too, remembering it eventually becoming much of what living it amounts to, in proportion to the time one has left to live it. Bill Burroughs is that way too, come to think, being as he is in his early to mid 80s, preferring, that is, to *live* life, preferably life on a stool, not only in the bar but *at* the bar, side by side with his interlocutor, conversing about the various things, or across from the charming Debbie Harry, exchanging pleasantries. But Neal Cassady not only believes in reincarnation, he believes in time travel too, and when he mentioned that, I asked him to give me a concrete example, not that I'm going to believe it or him, one way or the other

Sometimes you'd be sitting at the bar, maybe alone at first, there, conversing with your book, or stacks of books, moving from one to the other, checking out the *book-feel* of the book in question, reading a little and then reading across to the next one and so forth, and then someone would come in and take up the bar stool next to you, friend or stranger soon to become friend through conversation, and after being a ways into the evening, the conversation a-flowing, you'd spot a table occupied by a couple poets or three of them, carrying on about beer, the poets in this town being the brewers, or you'd spot the table occupied by the scientists, and you'd find yourself drawn their way, and so maybe you'd move there with them, your knowing them because your neighbor, Henry David, is a scientist, he there with his fellow biologists, fish biologists mostly, going on about cichlids and DNA and sticklebacks and such, or, in the case of the so-called microbe geeks, going on about microbial clouds and such, talking fecal matter, for example, and how we leave pools of butt-crobes in our seats when we leave them, or how our bodies, each with their own individuated microbial clouds, intermix with the microbial clouds of others and so forth, so sitting down there with them sharing microbiomes for a bit, taking in the DNA talk or the microbial talk or the stickleback research or talking climate crisis ("we're fucked" etc), but even then, you'd ask your bar-partner to save your chair, your bar-stool, actually more like a bar-chair, like a high chair for adults, and you'd leave your books and your journal or notebook there at the bar to reserve your coveted space at the bar, there being only six bar-chairs at the bar, sometimes seven, with the extra one squeezed in at the end by one of the transgressing regulars, you'd keep that stool taken so that, despite being drawn to one of the other tables, you'd not get too sucked in, however flowing the conversation, so you'd have an exit strategy should they invite you to stay at their table, your place being *at* the bar, not just *in* the bar but *at* it, however enticing the table full of scientists, the poets too, though, in this town, the poets are the brewers, me still being new to this town, not knowing where the poets of Eugene are to be found, finding them nowhere in sight

Our neighbor, Nazi Tim, as we call him, being a yard-nazi, forever blasting away with his yard machinery, mowing down the wild flowers and blowing yard matter about, into the street or into his neighbor's yard, or torching weeds or executing another tree or building yet another shed to house who-knows-what, firearms maybe, he being a Xian, naturally, and so stockpiling weapons for the coming purge maybe, he, Nazi Tim, pointed out to me today that my car was making weird clicking noises last night, or rather, early this morning. I had noticed it myself, I told him, after he described the sound. It's my car's locking system, whatever you call it, and I had been noticing the weirdness myself, just that day. You know, where the locks go back and forth, locking and unlocking, back and forth, now locked, now unlocked, click clack, not locked now unlocked and then locked again. So I start up the car and there it is, the clicking off and the clicking on sound, the sound of the locks clicking back and forth. WTF, I'm saying this morning, getting into the car and heading off to work. Clickety clack, clickety clack, like some kind of post-industrial, rhythm machine messing with my work-a-day head

Just back from the Stein, where I happily ran into George Harrison, who I had not seen for quite a while, and when I had seen him last, the last few times he had been with his wife and daughter. Not that I'm not into sitting down with his wife and daughter and talking but only that George Harrison and me had not had the chance to talk one on one for awhile. The first time it being about music, but also so much more that I cannot remember now. We had excellent conversation, per usual, but this one was one of those memorable ones that build a bond between the two interlocutors, not that I can remember it. Then I ran into Bob Creeley in the bathroom, which was a shock to our systems, since we had not seen each other in a while and that fact alone had caused us to think about the fact that we had not seen each other in a while, this being on both our minds, as it happens, because we occasionally see each other passing in our vehicles at our kids' middle school and wave and you can see it in each other's look that we really must get ourselves soon to a saloon, so to speak, or say at the Stein, and so that's what we said in the bathroom together. As it happens, Henry David and his fish gang from the university were there, including the Spaniard. They'd been there the whole time, talking fish, no doubt, whilst I was having this brilliant conversation with George Harrison about music and stuff I can't remember

I'm listing to PJ Harvey's new anti-war album, *Let England Shake,* on the way down from Portland, where I came upon the music in a store and swarmed down on it with my credit card, I played it back to back, three times over, driving from Portland to Eugene, even though I had the Robert Wyatt to listen to, also new to me, which I couldn't wait to get to, but obviously did, that is to say, I did wait to get to it, listening to Polly Jean instead, over and over, even though I was very anxious to get to the Wyatt, after reading about him in *Art Forum*. It was one of those musical products you grind into the ground, practically ruining the music, so obsessed with listening to it over and over again as you are. Speaking here of Polly Jean, if I may. All wrapped up in the way it connects you to the world, in that fresh way again, to what little "world" we have left, especially here in *The States*, until basically you've neutralized it, played it over and over and over and so now it's gone, something once so great, rocking your world, such that you want to tell everyone about it, write about it, for example, and then it's gone and you're thinking, WTF, where did that feeling go?

I have seen and done things I want to forget,
soldiers fell like lumps of meat,
blown and shot out beyond belief.
arms and legs were in the trees.

P.J. Harvey, "The Words That Maketh Murder"

The previous week, Sedgwick and I had been up from Eugene to Portland to see The Decemberists at Schnitzer Hall. The mayor of Portland Sam Adams was there and on the way out of the concert I crossed his path. He nodded to me, as I crossed his path, acknowledging my recognition of him as mayor and in effect appreciating that fact, as if to say, Hi, thank you for noticing me (even though I was just recognizing him right there and then, quickly, on my feet, having seen a picture of the man, once, but hearing a lot about him, lately, *the scandal*, whatever it is, on the radio, *and you've got the Lars Larson Show*, Lars Larson of course hating on the mayor because the mayor's a homo, openly he's homo, which the Lars Larson construction is not really against, supposedly, as a matter of principle, some of his best friends being homo, for instance, but not certainly for it, either, *as a way of life*, he'd likely say, the homo *lifestyle*, Lars being against that and all, there being a so-called homo lifestyle presumably, vs. a hetero lifestyle, naturally, the latter being natural, naturally, whilst the former abnormal, naturally, but then figuring it out, there and then, when our paths crossed in the theatre, having seen the people looking at him and shaking his hand before the show and figuring that's probably *the mayor*, enemy of Lars and the *Lars Larson Show*. But there was also this sense to his nod that we were both in a great place and time here and now at this moment. As if to say, isn't it great to be here in Portland at this beautiful theatre coming out fresh from a concert by Portland's own Decemberists on this beautiful evening with all these cool Portland people (hipsters, old and new alike) around us which includes you and me, the mayor, at this brief moment, this brief encounter, but not the likes of Lars Larson, certainly not Lars Larson

I've run into mayors before, like the one in Buffalo, also the one here in Eugene, and they always seem eager for you to notice them, they looking you in the eye, as if wondering, *You know who I am, right?* or, *I'm your mayor, you know that, right?*

Previous to the Stein I had been at the doctor's to get some blood pulled again. This time they're checking for hepatitis, trying to figure out why my liver's inflamed, or whatever they call it. I went on an alcohol fast for 12 days, which for me meant a beer fast and that meant the Stein too. But, happily, the liver failed to deflate. True, I did think at the time and even now in fact that it would have been a good thing, had my liver in fact de-inflated, since I can control my intake of beer and alcohol in general, according to how I like to think, though true I do have an addictive personality, according to the doctor, which is not to say that people are addicted to my personality but yet that my being (or character sketch) is prone to addictions. I'm prone, that is, to get hooked on things. I liked when she said that, saying that in her happy way, her bedside manner, so to say, because it made it seem beyond my control, like that was just who I am, as a person, just like when she told me, in her happy totally non-threatening way (or *bedside manner*), that, according to the machine, I had a seven percent chance of dying in the next twenty-five years, whereas here I thought I'd be dying any day now. That is to say, I am prone to getting hooked on pleasurable things, to find pleasure in patterns, in routines of pleasure, which in my case translates as: off work, head to the pub to celebrate the day and life in general, but also to celebrate being set free from work, for the day, though right there in fact celebrating it in the midst of workers working, bartenders drawing pints not so different than nurses drawing blood, come to think. In other words, I get off work and then head back to work, the bar, in this case, its being somebody else's workplace, and though me not working myself, me, in effect, back at work, even if not working myself, just me watching others work, sometimes conversing with the workers, sometimes flirting with the workers, men and women alike, conversation being all about flirtation, sometimes tipping the workers, sometimes complaining about the workers, judging their work and all, as if we were their supervisors, as if being off work ourselves we now get to dump on the workers just as we ourselves were just hours ago getting dumped on ourselves and so now wanting to dump on them in turn, it being *our turn*. And then each day being like that and going on like that forever. Addicted to buzz, I admit it, as I like transporting my body and mind to another place, another state of whatever being. Becoming hops, or becoming grapes, or becoming juniper berries, whatever, there are many flavors. Why stay in the same state, after all? Why not travel to this other state, from time to time, like a time traveler, which, for me, means, on a fairly regular basis, that is to say, every day, with each day being like that and going on like that forever? That is, until the liver shrivels up and chokes the life out of you. (Oh yeah, that.) So that traveling is part of your everyday life, part of your being, not some kind of vacation you wait around for the whole year, a measly week or two of transport or vacating and then back to the grind of work, there being nothing but work if there's no vacating, no time travel, there, side-by-side beside the working, the laboring, that is. Having spent a good chunk of my life abroad, I have plenty of practice traveling to other states of mind, free of the place I'm living, buzzed

This time it was Allen Ginsberg. I'd seen him seated at the Ken Babbs event at Tsunami Books, Babbs being a friend of Mary Prankster, our Eugene hero made into a statue, statue on a plinth. Ginsberg was seated a couple rows up from where I was standing. I didn't feel like fraternizing, given where he was seated, given that he was wedged in next to others and so their eyes surely scoping me out, imaginary or not, which I didn't feel like dealing with at the time, the scoping out but also the brushing up against the knees of the seated ones, and then the sitting next to Allen Ginsberg, and so having to listen to his jokes, which are Frog's jokes, Frog being Eugene's famous hippie jokester, bad jokes, to be sure, but then, given my fondness for bad jokes, that in and of itself not being the problem, just my not wanting to take in those jokes at the time or brush against the knees of the seated ones, not to mention the scoping out, imaginary or no, so I didn't bother to say hi. Today, when I ran into Allen Ginsberg at the Stein, he said he had seen me at Tsunami at the Babbs event and I explained that I too had seen him at Tsunami at the Babbs event. I told him I didn't stick around for it, even though I had this feeling this was some kind of historical event, Babbs being one of the Merry Pranksters, close friend of the late Ken Kesey, and, actually, it was my intent to go to the Babbs event and actually stay there for it. (By the way, I'm talking of the real Ken Babbs here, just as I'm talking about the real Ken Kesey here, unlike the fictional Allen Ginsberg, who is just a place-name employed to protect the guilty, just like the fictional Bill Burroughs, not to mention the fictional author him or herself.) I also said to Allen Ginsberg that I felt it was just good to go out and attend these kinds of events, to support the culture in your community and all, and that, as citizen of Eugene, we have a civic duty to attend such things and so forth, a civic duty that in many ways explains my commitment to the Stein, our public square, said I to Allen Ginsberg, Ginsberg shaking his head in agreement before launching into some sort of manic monologue, interspersed with the occasional bad joke, passed onto him by his famous housemate, Eugene's own Frog, joke-maker/pamphleteer extraordinaire. Unlike some, I like Allen Ginsberg's jokes, scripted by the legendary Frog, but I do have to stop him when he begins to launch into one of his songs, or some lyric by one of his folk heroes, which he's always on the verge of doing despite (or in spite) of my protestations, a persistence that I admire, Allen Ginsberg being one of a number of Eugene's folk heroes, being a folk singer himself to boot. As it happens, it also happened to be the day that the two games of the Final Four were being played and my favorite of the two games was on – the beginning of the second half beginning soon – between Butler and UConn – and so I was feeling divided, (though now that I think of it, I'm thinking WTF, Butler vs. UConn?! as if I cared for either team, or for sports in general, fuck sports, sports in the USA being like the opiate of the masses and so forth, not the kind of intoxication I condone, though, true, I'm prone to getting sucked in by it and the March madness, being an American*, that is to say, a hypocrite: *Do I contradict myself? Very well, then I contradict myself. I am large, etc.* Fortunately, I happened to cross paths with the Babbs in question who kindly nodded to me and I to him nodding kindly as well, and so I thought, okay, I've gotten what I've come for, attending such events as much for their social aspect as the reading itself, most of which I have a hard time concentrating on, one line after the other spawning a line of thought that drifts off and away from reading at hand. Given that I wasn't really into listening to the dude on the guitar, who was leading up to the Babb's gig, not that I don't value that, the folk guitar stuff, popular in these parts. I'll buy his book later, after all the brouhaha, said I to myself at the time. Meanwhile, I'll shoot home for the rest of the game, trading one historical event for another. Not that there's an equivalency going on here. As it happened, the second half proved to be historical only insofar as it was historically awful and hence entirely forgettable. But was it due to bad basketball or just damn good defense on Connecticut's part? That is the question the pundits are tossing around on the radio. Soon enough, all will be forgotten and we'll find ourselves in another season with another historical event to forget, if not forego

Having a half hour or so free, I click open the *Noch Ein at the Stein* file and then think "beer" and so head over to Henry David's to draw me a pint. Me thinking "beer" is like when George Clooney wakes up in *O Brother, Where Art Thou* and the first thing he says is "my hair." Me and Henry David (the scientist, fish guy), who live two houses down from each other, share a keg together. At first, it was Ninkasi and now it's Oakshire (formerly known as Willamette, which I preferred. "Oakshire," the name (not the beer, though) doesn't cut it for me, sounding like some kind of Hobbit thing, though, now I'm used to it and so don't mind it anymore, don't even think Hobbit, and so don't mind it, having become accustomed to it as a result of repetition and time. Besides, they had no choice but to change since "Willamette," damnit, had already been *taken*, copyrighted, the name owned, in other words, and hence no longer usable). I'm not so down on Ninkasi, as some people are, though, I admit, its success has made it feel less *special*, preferring failure, as I do. We find ourselves waxing nostalgic over the days when you just pulled up and ordered the refill of your corny keg directly from the workers. They'd say help yourself to a pint or something along those lines as we were waiting there for our cornies and maybe we'd get in a pint or two, totally free of charge, waiting there as we were for our cornies, nursing pints so not in a hurry, pints pulled directly from the spout, which we, on their invite, helped ourselves to. Now they have a tasting room/bar, with a beautiful patio, and you get a token for a free beer per corny, which they pour for you, keeping track of everything, as required by law

I'm not saying I'm against that (*progress*, and all, so-called) and that I don't want to see Ninkasi grow like that and succeed and all. Though, true, we're in Eugene, where by "growth" we usually mean "home grown." In fact, I take a bit of stake in the success myself, living vicariously as I do off of others' success. In fact, I prefer to piggyback rather than forge my own separate way. I like to skim off the success of others as a road to success myself, to ride their success as if it's mine too. I like to claim Ninkasi as one of Eugene's great successes and I ride on that, living as I do now in Eugene, just as you ride off of New York when you're living in Manhattan, like when you're at the old Knitting Factory, back in the day when it was right next to the legendary Milano's, and you're squeezed in there back in the day watching Bill Frisell meddling down there with the pedals, a squonk scrunching off the wah-wah as Joe Lovano bends into his sax like some kind of movie screen demon peeling off some kind of weirdness and Paul Motian tipping there the whole thing off balance with his off-kilter polyrhythms, his cymbalic-hesitations and the tom toms and the snare, de-snared, a-clunking clankily backwards then forwards down across to the floor tom, sliding off the side and then clumping momentarily onward, ahead of the beat then behind it, off to the side, above now below, sliding, no cymbals now. You live off that collective pride. It uplifts you. Finding one's self in the we-subjectivity of it all. That's real

The best hamburger I've ever had was at the golf course in Addis Ababa, Ethiopia. And it wasn't one I myself was eating. Let me explain. My brothers and I were out in the barn next to the clubhouse, where Mom and Dad were hanging out after eighteen, probably drinking a beer or two at the bar, perhaps a Shandy, which I thought was a cool idea for a drink at the time but which I now totally reject. Hanging with the other golfers, enjoying life, an international cast at the club. I can't remember what exactly was in the barn, except that there was hay up in the attic space. Maintenance equipment, most likely, lawnmowers and such down below. We were either up there ourselves, or we were down on the ground floor, but suddenly we noticed one of the Ethiopian caddies huddled in on himself, trying to hide from view. Realizing that we had seen him and then realizing that we had discovered his secret, that he was scarfing down a cheeseburger with an orange or grape Fanta or some other brand of bottled product, he smiled and put his finger to his mouth, signaling for us to remain quiet about his presence lest he be caught. It dawned on us, then, that the Ethiopian caddy had probably stolen the food, or, more likely, one of the cooks at the clubhouse had covertly slipped the food to the caddy, perhaps as a friendly gesture. Or, more likely still, there was this common practice among the Ethiopian staff at the golf course of passing on favors here and there when the occasion arose. Poaching off the colonialists, the *ferenges*, as they called us. In that sense, they were no different than any other worker, helping themselves to everyday perks whenever possible, taking a pen home from work, for example. It's not your pen, yet you take it, the thief that you are. What I remember most from that moment was the way the young man, Ethiopian, a caddy, was eating the cheeseburger, taking large bites from the cheeseburger, which was loaded up with the various accoutrements, dripping with that wonderful white cheese that I've never been able to find anywhere else in the world, though surely it was a specific kind of cheese, most likely Italian, and so surely I could find out what it was if I really looked into it. Anyway, the way his jaws bit down into the chewy bun and burger, through the cheese and condiments, and the way his tongue maneuvered the burger around in his mouth, working his cheeks, savoring every chomp, the burst of flavors, the bursting cheese, the somewhat rubbery texture of it squeaking against his teeth, the tangy flavor which mixed perfectly with the burger, and then the way he'd tilt back the Fanta bottle, slurping it down often while his mouth was still full of food, the liquid guzzling down his windpipe, then wiping his mouth with the back of his hand

I've been reading Kathy Acker's *My Mother: Demonology, a novel.* I picked up a hardback edition at Tsunami, with a red cover jacket and a photo of a sidewalk with a patch of grass in the middle where it forks off into two narrower sidewalks, such that, after a first glance or two, you realize it looks like a woman's vagina, a nice v-shaped hairy patch, (the hair being part of the vagina, according to Eve Ensler in the *Vagina Monologues*), not the rectangular designer patches we find today. Lester Bowie, one of the bartenders at the Stein, got a kick out of it. He picked up the book, curious about what I was reading, perhaps the patch had caught his eye, the patch of grass, and the first page he cracked it open to had a line with the word "pussy" or "cunt" in it, as you'd expect from Kathy Acker. I told him I preferred the word "snatch," as Marianne Faithful sings it, though Sedgwick, my wife, prefers "cunt," likes to say cunt now and then, usually out of sight in the family room where we sit alone watching *teevee*, as the poet Eileen Myles spells it. Is there any good word for these things these days, somehow the words distort the things themselves, heavy with history, heavy with flesh, even genitals sounds degrading, though delicious in a kind of sour way, too, like a good sour. I mean I don't mind slurping on some genitals, to be frank, or on sours, for that matter. I myself like all the words for it, in the end, the thing in question, not to mention the thing itself. Just yesterday I came across "snatch" in Ted Berrigan's *Sonnets*, as if I was destined to find it, though, once it sees you, you see snatch everywhere

Snatch is English, I think, the British way of saying cunt, not that they don't say cunt aplenty, or maybe that's just because I think of Marianne Faithful when I hear the word, who I saw the other day in Jean Luc Godard's *Made in the U.S.A.* In Godard's *U.S.A.* there's this passage where the narrator or one of the characters goes through a list of sentences that don't make any sense, the subject and predicate all messed up, each of Godard's sentences proving, via some kind of Wittgensteinian language game, that language cannot be reduced to the instrumental, that it's not all just about making sense. That there's this excess in language, something left over after sense has driven home its point, conducted its business, though not in fact *left over* since sense is only made possible by language's excess, right? I feel like the language forced me into saying that. In any case, it made me wonder whether this passage in *U.S.A.* was one of the influences on Language poetry. The title of Charles Bernstein's "Three or Four Things I Know About Him" coming from Godard's *Three or Four Things I Know About Her*, which is from the same period of films as *U.S.A.* So one presumes Charles had seen that, as probably had his peers, more or less. Just a thought

Neal Cassady, who is one cool customer, came in and sat on the stool next to me and so got in on the conversation. Neal Cassady and Lester Bowie both being what they used to call "ladies' men," but only insofar as many women are drawn to them, Neal Cassady being one cool customer, just like Lester Bowie, who's not only a cool customer, even when he's bartending, but a champion hugger, as well. I mentioned how I liked the bushiness of the would-be snatch on Acker's cover, though, in fact, it was just a patch of lawn, and that I longed for the days of the bushy lawn. We talked of how the women today were into shaving their snatches, and Neal

Cassady said he liked it when they shaved it into a somewhat thin rectangle and we both agreed that that was nice, even though I was making the opposite point. I had in mind that bushy thing in that late 90s movie by Bernardo Bertolucci, I think it was his film but I'm not sure, where the young Italian woman takes off her clothes and there's this healthy, wild patch of dark pubes all thick and wild and wicked and the man, seated on the bed, sticks his face in it, her hands in his lush Italian hair

Sometime I return to this project in my mind's eye while driving and I imagine myself as one of the characters in some would-be film script I'm making up on the spot, in this case the character who's driving the car, the protagonist that is, and that what I'm seeing out my windshield—the Eugene cityscape washing by, good as any place to write about—is what the camera sees and that the music streaming out my stereo is the film's soundtrack, and that I as a character, driving the car and listening to said music, which happens to be on the character's said car stereo, having just come from visiting with said friend, say at the said Stein, making the friends I've made at the Stein characters in the film, as it were, and that this film, being that it takes place in Eugene, and in fact was once titled "Eugene," at least it was until I changed it to *Noch Ein at the Stein*, the latter translated in my pidgen German as "Another One at the Stein," though it literally translates as "Another at the stone," and that this film in question is like in the Kerouac mode, wherein the characters are jumping around from here to there, partying at so and so's house, did Kerouac ever come to Eugene, one wonders, waking up with a group hangover, a group of guys (naturally), and then heading over to Brails for breakfast, coffee, maybe a Bloody Mary to go along with it, three eggs, sausage or bacon or both, biscuits and gravy maybe (though nobody in this town does biscuits and gravy right, save Jiffy Market, though they serve it out of a can, I've heard, and a good can at that, in my mind, given that those who make it from scratch have it totally wrong, totally wrong everywhere I go in Eugene, save that can at the Jiffy), hash browns, toast, and so forth, or it'd be like in the John Cassevettes mode, maybe black and white, lots of guys running around from here to there, talking the whole time, a bunch of husbands, white husbands in black suits and white shirts, and tie, early-sixties style, saying some sexists things, grabbing after women in a bar or café, each of the characters or two of them doing the majority of the talking, trying to outdo each other, like in the *Big Lebowski*, drinking and smoking, Eugene being the Dude's kind of town. In fact, if there's one town or city that embodies the Dude's ethos, it is Eugene

The Stein's the kind of establishment that understands the importance of a good glass, that certain beers demand certain glasses. Even when somebody buys a bottle from their voluminous racks, the bartenders do not hesitate to pour the bottled contents into its proper glass, some quite particular for its exacting kind of beer, unless the customer, foolishly, to be sure, indicates otherwise. As a rule, one does not drink from a bottle at the Stein, just as one does not drink industrial beer at the Stein, as there is no industrial beer to be had at the Stein, though occasionally some industrial beer guy stumbles in, wanders in off the street like some kind of dumb-ass, and asks for some dumb-ass industrial beer, without glass, naturally, a tall-neck, say

I'm going to have to amend my claim that Eugene is entirely absent as a cultural force, with respect to the rest of the country and the world, what with Eugene being at the forefront of the environmentalist movement, not to mention home to the so-called eco-terrorists, monkey-wrenching the profits of logging companies and torching SUVs (Sports Utility Vehicles), back in the day, at least. But also, there's the great beer, you know, and then there's great wine, you know, and then there's the whole locavore thing, which, of course, it's a major part of, though, true, I guess that's part of the hippy legacy, and then there's the whole bicycle thing and the running thing, Tracktown USA, and of course the weed and the has-been hippy legacy thing itself, still in evidence, however neutralized, that is to say, neoliberalized by the hippycrits, keeping, of course, the beer thing and the wine thing and the weed thing and the organic food thing and cycling thing and the tracktown thing and capitalizing on the eco thing, but ditching the communist horizon, the communist horizon mowed down like clear-cuts, a horizon once there, now chewed up like the flora and fauna, the undergrowth done in and so forth. One-time hippies gone capitalists, now rolling in the dough, yet still spinning "away the dew" at the Country Fair and such, but as a cultural force actively on the world's stage, I was thinking it's like *not really there* (even if there's plenty of there here), being overshadowed by Portland, most immediately, with California lurking below and Seattle, not to mention Vancouver, up in the Canada (not Vancouver, Washington, needless to say, which is like Portland's New Jersey). Yet, upon further reflection, thought stoked by the embers of loafing, loafing at the Stein, say, I reassessed, thinking Eugene may be *the* new cultural force, so laid back it's hardly noticeable, loafing being where it's at, the wave of the future, what with climate carnage breathing down our necks, the smoke at our throats, forcing upon us the rigors of Eugene's anti-productivist ethos (save the hippycrits), if only we'd stop and loaf and take it all in, the coming extinction event creeping up on us as if unawares, catching us off-guard, if not in denial, as if surprised

Poetic Interlude: Eugene, City of Loafers

People outside, enjoying the loafing, loafing, say, in the many parkways of South Eugene, though their taking the dog on the walk, in say the dog park, serves a function, given the dog's confinement in the apartment or house or yard all day long, and so no, not an instant of loafing, after all not at all.

But the place where dog and human loose themselves in the walking, that's what I'm talking about, that's where the loafing begins, intentionally or not, where they transcend their function, getting loose, not fit, though perhaps fit as a bonus to their loosening, a bonus track.

There at Kesey Square, you'll find the loafers, loafing amid the food carts, taking it easy for all us winners, begging for money sometimes, other times playing guitars, maybe bongo, when you look like someone to beg from, a pungent sneer as

you pass them by, no change trickling
down, a calculated gesture, hard fought.

There's a gourmet donut place right there,
near the square, the square dedicated to
an acid head, a working-class loafer.

Lots of neo-hippies junking up the place
with their stink, jeering at the taxpayers.
Hey, you! You gotta buck, I'm hungry, bitch,
goes their pitch, slouching there on the
steps like a bunch of punk-ass pseudo-
loafers.

"Can't they round 'em up and pack 'em
out, eminent domain their spunk out of
here, they and their stinky ways?" – this
part, plus the stanza above, written as if
I'm some kind of Lars Larson talk radio
host, *and you've got the Lars Larson Show.*

And you looking like someone to beg
from, Mr. Nine Eleven.

At the Saturday Market there's plenty of loafing, or is it selling disguised as loafing, selling stuff they made themselves, crafts, potions, people playing acoustic stuff, bongo, acting like hillbillies, organic food for sale, flowers—"Why grow them if you can't eat them?" (Granddad)—protecting their ground, their corners—*Back off, intruder!*

The Country Fair, like some kind of faux Middle Ages like village, a sort of Disney version of the Dark Ages, like the Middle Ages but without the darkness, running through the trippy trees with our ponies, our little stub of sword, the Shire or something, in our robes, loosely fit garments, leggings, folks telling tales, tales of lore, juggling and hippyshit like that, spinning around, tits painted as daisies, old guys with their balls hanging out, sweaty ball sack and all, reeking of patchouli and sweat. Fair-junkies dreaming about a full time Country Fair, every day every year, wouldn't it be cool if we could just like live like this forevermore? Imagining it in their mind's eye like some kind of movie but without the usual, if not inevitable, slide into dystopianism.

Where the fantasy is full time, yet a real way to stumble down the street, that's really livable for real; please, let me be, I'm dreaming, don't wake me, go away, *let it blossom, let it glow.*

Yet even here we find a symptom, like some kind of conqueror worm.

The consumers—those who pay to play— walking around in circles looking at crafts and things to buy, and the producers— those who pay and some who're paid to get in or who volunteer their services to get in, who then get to really party down when all the consumers leave, after the capitalism dies down, getting naked in the bath house, for example, doing the drugs and drinking the good beer, some of the finest in the world made right here in Eugene and surrounds, tripping and having free sex or something, getting hippy-like, let's do this.

Or just hanging at a table in Jiffy Market, reading the paper, sharing sections with other tables, and the people sitting there at them, they screwed up when they put the flat screen up there, peering down there in the middle of the things down our back sides, where the news gets in, wine bottles to the right, groceries in rear, the deli to the left, cash register and row of coffee thermoses in front, Doug's Nuts at the counter among chocolates, coffee beans, and other stuff to purchase, cigarettes, for example, the cash register, ordering a biscuits and gravy (from a can, freshly opened, a fine can) or ordering a half of hot pastrami and swiss cheese on marbled rye fully dressed, for example.

Then there's the antithesis of loafing, The Highlands, a large bar, with pool

tables and ping pong tables, and tables
for parties, and booths, each with their
individuated mini-flatscreens, just ask
them and they'll plug you into anything
you want, they have, I believe, from
memory, a total of seven sets of booths,
with red faux-leather seating, cracked
in places, the yellow foam bulging out,
crumbling, lumpy here and crumbly
there like some kind of cheesy disease,
and then, of course, its being a sports bar,
TV sets floating around, above and below,
everywhere you go, up your backside or
in your face, basically, they have darts
and some pinball machines, as well a
basketball game or, *hoops*, where you
try to score as many baskets as possible
within a minute or so, sometimes I'll be
sitting there loafing, reading with beer
at hand, at hand and then in hand, then
hand to mouth, and suddenly somebody
will decide to shoot some hoops, making
racket, bells and whistles, the clank
of ball on rim, some groovin' music in
the background, often times great stuff

like James Brown or Curtis Mayfield or other times cheesy bad stuff, like AC/DC, or Guns and Roses, things the artists like, poets getting off on liking them, pretending they really like AC/DC, for example, and such, and feeling good about it, honestly, like getting off on Bread or something like The Carpenters or America's "Muskrat Love," folding them into a poem or two, mixing it in with crowd sounds from a basketball game or football, that and real live people sounds, plus there are slot machines around the back, near the ATM and the cigarette machine, some gamblers slouching there in chairs, slamming at the keys.

And then there's the Eugene drivers just sauntering along, loafing, in their vehicles, loafingly lollygaggling along, puttering about at 20 mph or so, dipping down to around 15 or 12 around corners, cars lined up in back, some in a hurry, dipping left to see who's in front slowing things down, getting stuck behind the loafers in their Priuses, lollygaggling or dawdling, puttering along in their hydro-electricity culled from some dam, near or far, causing the drivers in back in their jacked up trucks or minis to swerve left to see who's holding things up, the East Coasters and the Californistas or the flag flappers from Springfield, going bonkers, dipping left, dipping right, bumpered up, trying to win the day, jacked up in their suspension, torqued out, aching to get somewhere, shoving people out of the way, yet slowed down by the loafers, forced to do so, swerving left then peeking right to see what's holding things up.

And what about the old folks who hang out in the early mornings at Barry's Bakery, hanging out around a table, talking about this and that, not averse to talking politics, for example, drinking coffee and eating coffee cake or eating a toasted bialy with cream cheese and locks and such, a slice of quiche say, getting in the way of those in a hurry, the older folks not in a hurry, wanting to linger, not adverse to talking about the various things, sitting around a table talking, finally here in the final years, getting round to it, round to the talking, not averse to talking politics, for example.

Everyone everywhere jogging or running, young and old and middle agers, white humans in a white town, jogging or running around the Amazon Parkway, jogging or running on the soft paths, paved with wood chips and soft such, a springy taxpayer feel to it, like you're walking on someone's back, taxpayers money running up and down Spencer Butte, or busy running down along the river, out to where the mall is or out toward Springfield, Eugene's New Jersey, not exactly loafing, to say the least, busy running, getting fit, taxpayers ganja, feeling healthy, alive-like, not running somewhere, as mode of transportation, rather running to get fit, to defy death, to live forevermore, to own it and the body as bonus, you look great, thanks.

And then the cyclists, who are forever getting in the way of the vehicles and their road, using the road as if it was theirs, these cyclists, who are always and forever breaking the rules, riding through a stop sign, for example, or sometimes riding on sidewalks, who then end up shoving the walkers around, walkers who've just gotten out of their cars, say, and then are suddenly banging up against a cyclist, a cyclist who then runs a red light, practically running over a walker who moments ago stepped out of a car.

Many of those loafers lollygaggling along in their vehicles are not in fact loafing, or loafers, these kind of Eugenians are effectively trying to force upon the others their driving habits and their ideology of slow driving, trying to get across to their fellow drivers the importance of being a safe, that is, slow driver, a civic driver, looking out for pedestrians (humans) and cyclists (resources), but even more so, trying to get across the importance of slowing down, of not being in a hurry, going slow, and that if we could all just slow down, society would be so much better, yet taking great pleasure in producing the tension behind them, the car that creeps up on their fender, that rides their tale gate, jazzed up on caffeine, late for something, swerving left and right and riding them, getting tense, jacked up on torque value, and taking pleasure in that, making them feel that way for their own good, *it's for your own good!*

So my plan was to play the new High Llamas album on the drive to the poker party at our lawyer friend Charlie Reznikoff's house in order to get some feedback from Henry David and, particularly, Bob Creeley, see what they thought about this unusual group that no one I knew seemed to know about, much less *get* or care about or even like, including Sedgwick, she and I usually sharing our tastes. So I slipped the cd into the car stereo as Henry David and I drove off to Bob Creeley's house to pick him up, eager to share it, though waiting until Bob was in our presence to push "play." But when we arrive at his house, Bob Creeley comes running out looking panicked and confused: he lost his wallet, he tells us, and so can't come to the poker party until he finds it. (As it turned out, he left it at the bar a couple hours earlier and, amazingly, it was still there two hours later, just sitting there on the ledge, ledge or windowsill.) So Bob tells us he'll have to drive to Rezy's himself and that he'd see us later, hopefully soon. I yell out that if he's truly lost his wallet, rather than say, misplaced it at home due to booze or weed, that he'll want to call the bank, credit card companies, etc., as if he didn't know that

So we drive away, me disappointed because I was looking forward to the three of us heading off together and to my debuting the new High Llamas album *Talahomi Way* for them, before, that is, we arrived at Donny's house to pick him up. I was especially eager for Bob Creeley's feedback, wanting to listen to the music again but through his ears this time, because the last time we were all together, which was at our house for a game of euchre, I played *Snowbug* and Bob Creeley *got it*, unlike Henry David—though, true, Henry David later claimed otherwise. Sedwick, unlike Henry David, made no pretense, just remained silent, putting up with yet another of my attempts at conversion. I didn't really believe Henry David, given his tendency to go along with things, at least at that point in our friendship, rather than being brutally honest like Sedgwick tends to be, long-married as we are and all, though, she has always been like this, a quality that drew me to her, having myself grown up in a family that repressed things. So, me not really believing Henry David that night, the euchre night, though appreciating his feigned endorsement, whilst Bob Creeley and I delighted over various musical moves on the part of the High Llamas, laughing at key passages (arrangements), taking them kind of ironically, true, though I was telling Bob Creeley and Henry David that I didn't think they were being ironic, or rather, yes, they're being ironic but only in the way the music's unapologetic beauty seems ironic *at first*—luscious strings and twirling harp, the urban vibraphones and trembling marimbas, bass as well as harmony clarinets, golden nylon guitar picking and perky banjo, with slapstick horns thrown in here and there at adroit moments, not to mention the electronic bleeps and the cantering clatter of percussion (not the usual steady drum kit holding down a four-four beat)—a *supposed* irony, then, that on further listening reverses itself, such that what at first seemed ironic turns out to be an earnest hailing after beauty, the unapologetically, if retro-sounding, giving-over to melody, suggesting that the irony felt by the uninitiated ear was simply one's own (historically determined) discomfort with a radicalized beauty, The High Llamas, for the so-called *sophisticated* ear, seeming out of step with the times, which, true, they may seem to be, but that's the whole point, what makes them radical, they in fact aiming for that, the music jolting us out of the continuous present of our just-in-time lives, forcing us (or inviting us) to recognize and then pass through the distancing forces still within us, though, true, still stuck here in our current, humorless, neo-Victorian stink hole, I could use the return of some irony, a treated-irony, to be sure, that of good cheer, decidedly not of the ol' snarky cliquish variety

So we're driving away from Bob Creeley's house heading off to pick up Donny and I'm a little disappointed, but Henry David and I soon find ourselves laughing again, having picked up on my earlier comment that this scenario—us heading off to pick up Bob and then Donny—was making me feel like we were in one of the *Hangover* scenes, me saying "this is feeling eerily like a scene from *The Hangover*," both of us having recently watched the flick on cable, Henry David saying, yeah, he was actually thinking that himself, as if our minds were in a mind-meld or something, both of us then agreeing that Bob Creeley would have to be the dentist character, not to say that his wife is anything like the dentist's uber-nasty fiancé—it's a guy's film, what do you expect?—adding that, if Bob Creeley was the dentist, then I guess I'm the fat guy, me offering that, making Henry David the suave, if not sexy, schoolteacher (Henry not minding being compared to the studly Bradley Cooper). So, anyway, we circled back to pick up Donny, both of us agreeing that Donny would be the guy that's missing, and hence largely out of the picture, insofar as Donny's not in our picture that often in real life, as it happens. *Shut the fuck up, Donny.*

So, as Henry David hustles up the steep steps to Donny's hill-side house to fetch Donny—they, like us, living in the "High Lands" or *South Hills* of Eugene—I cue up a song from the High Llamas' new album *Talahomi Way*, the title referring to some imaginary neighborhood, just getting underway, that gets stalled or something, the neighborhood being part of a larger, utopian-like community in a southern-Cal-like place that runs out of money and so never materializes. It's the name of a street there, right? Near the beach or something. "Take my hand and run it through the sand." A street with no houses or buildings, just the promise of a coming community. Anyhow, for some reason, the usually chronically terse Donny, when he gets in the car, becomes a Chatty Chucky and so I can't get the High Llamas in edgewise, wanting at least to get some feedback from Henry David, Bob Creeley being out of the picture, sadly, and me not necessarily caring much about what Donny thinks, in this case, though Donny does indeed, for a fact, have some good tastes, along the lines of stuff we both like

So we're pulling away from Donny's house, heading down the street toward the steep hill that, on the way out there, I had had to downshift into first gear to get up, and there's Donny jabbering away about a story he was apparently dying to tell us, just like I was dying to play them the new High Llamas, wanting to jabber on about how bizarrely different they are from any other pop group around, as far as I know, save perhaps Stereolab, their being the obvious connection, the Llamas' Sean O'Hagan having once been in the band, not to mention that Stereolab's Tim Gane produced *Talahomi Way*, though Stereolab is totally hip whilst the band The High Llamas is totally square, though in a totally radically hip way and so forth. And then when the High Llamas finally does come on, due to my having pushed "play," finally at last having the chance to draw their attention to it, saying how wonderfully different and happy the music is and so forth, giddily-loquacious-Donny just shoots it down—*Are you kidding me? What the fuck is this?*—brushing it aside and proceeding on with his chattering, being as he is a Chatty Chucky tonight, and me thinking maybe I like the typically terse Donny instead

Yesterday was one of those classic evenings at The Stein. At first I sat at the very end of the bar, alone, with my book, and a pint of Firestone Walker Double Jack Double IPA, with a whopping 9% alcohol, which was dangerous since the beer was so good. I had just come from the University of Oregon's Library with a new book to dive into: Peter Clark's *The English Alehouse: A Social History, 1200-1830*. I was quite pleased with my new find. It suddenly dawning on me that hanging out at The Stein was itself a form of loafing and, to be frank, one of my favorite forms and favorite sites of loafing. Insofar as being the self-appointed Director of the Institute of Loafing, it dawned on me that I should research the history of bars and pubs, which is how I ended up with Clark's book—just the sort of thing I was looking for, working as I've been at *The Institute of Loafing*, one of my other summer writing projects (of which the above, a small sample, preview, if you will). As it happens, the book, placed on the bar, cover up this time, introduced me to Peter, the track coach from Oxford, who noticed and asked about the book, not noting that his name too was Peter, which, had he done so, pointing it out, that is, wouldn't have been very English of him, so I pointed it out as being a nice coincidence, or "cowinkadink," as one of the characters in the new version of *Perry Mason* put it—this being an instance of what I call a poetics of implosion, wherein the writer, when revising, adds things from within, regardless of whether they interrupt the flow of the narrative, or whether they disrupt the chronological order of the text, comments from the future now embedded in what is presently the past tense of the writing, the current moment reading makes of all writing—Peter, who proved to be an accomplished conversationalist, and a lover of a good pint or two, our talk ranging from the quality of Pacific Northwest beer in comparison to England's beer (less alcohol and so more consumption, and so, me thinking this while he was saying it, more loafing at the bar) to track to living in Oxford versus Eugene now to Brighton, where I spent my last year in England, I told him, mentioning The Greys, my favorite pub there, a small place, kind of like the Stein not to mention Milano's, the conversation weaving this way and that, never faltering the whole time, me talking about the many good pubs in Brighton, mentioning The Greys again, a cozy, crowded place, where many a shoulder did rub, conversation rolling and weaving and swerving and so forth, and he, Peter, going on about some pubs in Oxford and London, me mentioning that pub in Camden Town, before the new owners spruced things up and drove away all the regulars, and so forth

Later, it struck me how Peter, the track coach from Oxford, differed from the kind of track fanatics you meet here in Eugene, where the latter are always and a day going on about their running, how many miles they've been running, going on about this marathon or going on about this or that mini-marathon, the relay marathon from Mount Hood to the Oregon coast, how they're going to run in the Boston Marathon this year, how their spouse went the previous year and so it's now their turn, and so forth, whereas Peter, the Oxford track coach, hardly ever discussed track or running unless you asked him about it and then he was rather matter of fact about it, discussing maybe the politics of this or that tournament, or the difference between track here in Eugene and track there in Oxford or in Australia, where he also works, but that most of the time the Oxford track coach Peter conversed about everything other than track, from talking beer to talking politics to talking about the new stadium at the University (not a fan), talking about Nike's influence on the University and on the town of Eugene (not a fan), which, granted, is still related to track, track and field, but is nothing like the ongoing and never-ending, self-congratulatory chatter about running and marathons, mini-marathons too, the Hood to Coast Relay, talking work outs, talking weight, talking diet, talking equipment, talking shoes, talking injuries, talking step counts, talking calories, talking about their new Apple watch and their heart rate and such, saying nothing about beer, saying nothing about politics, nothing about travel, nothing about other places, nothing about literature, nothing about movies, nothing about cooking, having nothing of that, these Eugene runners who, unlike Peter, always make it known that they are runners and so forth

Then I think about loafing again and I recall the passage in Max Weber's *The Protestant Ethic and the Spirit of Capitalism* where Weber's going on about merchants, the putter-outers, preferring to work less, as tradition had it, putting in a handful of hours or so, and then heading to the tavern for some beer and conversation, rather than working more hours for extra cash, rather than trying to *grow* the business, this before "the traditionalist spirit" gave way to "the spirit of capitalism":

> The number of business hours was very moderate, perhaps five to six a day, sometimes considerably less; in the rush season, where there was one, more. Earnings were moderate; enough to lead a respectable life and in good times to put away a little. On the whole, relations among competitors were relatively good, with a large degree of agreement on the fundamentals of business. A long daily visit to the tavern, with often plenty to drink, and a congenial circle of friends, made life comfortable and leisurely. (66-7)

This passage here explaining why I ended up with Peter Clark's *The English Alehouse: A Social History, 1200-1830*, which led to my meeting Peter, the track coach. Of course, when it comes to loafing, the problem with bars is that you tend to get drunk in them, which is fine while you're *in* the bar, the Stein, wherever, drinking the brews, our good, locally grown Northwestern beer, to be sure, the hoppy IPAs and all that, the reds, the ambers, the ales and the sours and the stouts and barley wines, and it's fine for a while afterwards too, but if you start too soon in the day, the rest of the day is basically a waste, heading to bed around 8:30 say, and then waking in the middle of the night, parched and heavy with piss, bloated like pig, swearing again you'll never do it again. As a loafer, you want to avoid that, the hangover part. Which is why I prefer to limit my drink in the bar to two or, at most, five pints, except when I occasionally go for four, or three-and-a-half or, say, less than seven. At the Stein, when you're kicking back IPA's like the Firestone mentioned earlier, three's enough to launch you into the zone. Which is why sometimes it's better to go to The Highlands, where the IPA's are more moderate (i.e. diluted if not entirely flat)—though, true, I've lately been thirsting for Ninkasi's Tricerahops Double IPA, which is 8.8% alcohol, the latter being on tap at the aforementioned establishment (i.e. The Highlands)

"Tricerahops is double everything you already love in an IPA. More hops, more malt body and a higher gravity define this Double India Pale Ale. Fiercely flavorful, guaranteed to satisfy." (Advertisement)

Firestone once being where it's at, though, implosively speaking, that is, this here passage being written long after the above passage, that day's long gone, just as Sticky Hands, while still being totally awesome, has been eclipsed by the whole East Coast Hazy IPA phenom—East Coast Hazies being a West Coast thing, as a matter of a fact, not so prominent back East, I've been told, which raises the question, *Why are they called East Coast Hazies when they appear to be a West Coast thing*—a trend which suddenly, seemingly out of nowhere (actually Vermont), descended upon the Eugene community some six months ago, such that everywhere one goes now, the loafers are babbling on about it endlessly, including those who turn their noses up at the hazies, being a trend and all, *their* trend being not to follow the trend. Of course, the really refined beer aficionados are long past the IPA craze and, though they appreciate those of us who remain stuck in our ways, being prone to habits and the glories of repetition, speaking here personally, they more or less look down on those who remain in the IPA camp as unsophisticated, even if once too they were way deep in the IPA camp, maybe even hazies included

As for sours, it's as if no one sours on sours, perhaps because they *are* sour, and because their tart ways are smart on the stomach—if you drink too many—which is perhaps why those into sours do not sour on sours, as sours are something one nurses, rather than slurping back like an IPA, though, true, the first IPA tends to go down slowly, similar to martinis in that sense—but after the first one's down the slurping begins

So I mentioned to Bill Burroughs the other day at the Stein this passage I read in Zizek's *In Defense of Lost Causes,* but I couldn't remember the quote exactly at the time and so had to paraphrase it at the time, but here it is in the flesh: "God has no positive content, the signifier merely positivizes our ignorance." So we talked about that, with me attempting to explain it and then Bill Burroughs trying to explain it back to me from what he could tell of my garbled attempt at explaining it to him, given that I didn't have the actual sentence before me, at the time, but yet a rather garbled paraphrase of it, us going back and forth like that for a time. This led to me trying to attempt to explain Wittgenstein and the twentieth century "turn to language" and all and so I was talking about Wittgenstein's line "the limits of my language mean the limits of my world," though I likely garbled it as well, perhaps reversing its syntax very likely, and I could tell that Bill Burroughs had not really thought of the ways in which language *is* our being and that there's no getting outside of language, as even when outside language one is *using* language to get outside it, which means one is inside language when outside it, outside it and therefore in it, though, on the other hand, I said to Bill Burroughs, one might be inclined to say that there may be an outside to our language, the language of the humans, that is, that we may or may not tap into without our knowing, merging perhaps with the language of trees, for example, like the feeling you get when in a stand of trees, I said to Bill Burroughs, or squirrel language, like the feeling you get when amongst the squirrels, Bill Burroughs bridling a bit at this line of thought and so I said, but what do I know and how would we know when knowing means language, the language of the humans, in our case, there side-by-side with a stand of trees, their roots conversing about this and that, entangled, amid the syntax of squirrels running up and down the said trees, not to mention worm talk and insect talk in general. I could tell that this line of thinking was news to Bill Burroughs because, at first, at least, it was like a light went off in Bill Burroughs's mind's eye, Bill Burroughs's mind's eye as it was thinking through the outward expressions of his body, which I noticed. In any case, I was very pleased at the sight of Bill Burrough's mind flashing its language about like some kind of virus, not that my mind wasn't flashing too. The light being language, language lighting Bill Burroughs's mind, his body lit by language, isn't the brain itself language, the way words have their way w/ u

Are you still in language, I said to myself, later, when you slip off above and away from your body toward the light? One wonders. Perhaps death is to be absented of language, thought I to myself, free at last of words, of searching always for the right words, words cleansed of their earthly residue, or words cleansed of their commercial residue and restored to their earthy ways, while the journey to the light itself is just language doing its thing till it runs out of letters, the letters that spell "light," the hard "t" being the last of it, or are there soft, cozy vowels waiting for us on the other side, on the far side of nothing, said I to myself thinking about what I had said to Bill Burroughs the other day

And then, later, today, that was yesterday or the day before, I read some more of Zizek, after reading Paul Clark's book on alehouses some, and I came across this passage, speaking of Deleuze: "'That the shade of pink has changed in an identifiable way is not all-important. It is that the change is a sign of a rearrangement of an infinity of other actual and virtual relations'" (321). This bringing to mind our discussion of Wittgenstein's discussion of color, as a way of explaining the contingency of meaning, using an example drawn from my own experience, and conveying this to Bill Burroughs the other day, who was willing to listen, listen to me trying make sense of stuff I didn't fully understand myself: I was on the back deck of our house in Louisville, Kentucky reading the *Philosophical Investigations*, one of the parts on color, when I noticed that the neighbor's otherwise greenish-brown fence was now blue, thanks to the reflection of the kiddy pool the neighbor had set up for his visiting grandson and the sun's bouncing the blue off the water. So I said to Bill Burroughs, would it be correct to say that the neighbor's fence is blue when usually it is greenish-brown? And so we talked about that for a bit

"Pleasure, which is fundamentally the intensified awareness of reality, springs from a passionate openness to the world and love of it. Not even the knowledge that man may be destroyed by the world detracts from the 'tragic pleasure.'" (Hannah Arendt, *Men in Dark Times* 6)

"We are all being used. I don't think you can make money in this country and not be used." (Kathy Acker, Wednesday @ 4-plus 1995 at PennSound, the final segment, on Burroughs's doing a Nike ad.)

I hadn't seen Bill Burroughs at the Stein for quite some time, which, due to his age and to Wally's sudden passing, made me wonder whether he too had perished. But I ran into him, finally, a couple days ago, sitting at the end of the bar, head buried in his new smart phone. Because Allen Ginsberg was also at the bar and because Bill Burroughs was engrossed in his new gadget, I chose to sit next to Allen Ginsberg, even though that meant sitting through his jokes, or rather Frog, his roommate's jokes, Allen Ginsberg laughing after each one of them while drumming his hands on the bar, and so it took some time for Bill Burroughs to notice me, looking up from his smart phone, at last, and giving me a brief smile before ducking his head back into the thing. I noticed that not only had Bill Burroughs's demeanor changed, but that his posture had, as well, such that his body was now slouched into a curved, almost hunchback, position resembling that of the letter "C," his head tilted down, slumped over the phone, which seemed like an extension of his body. We find a similar posture among our citizenry all over the place now, someone walking down the street, staring at this little box cupped in hand, the other hand's fingers rattling away at something, someone at a seat in a café doing the same, and so forth, everywhere, people curling in on themselves

So Lester Bowie draws me a Pliny the Younger, or was it Pliny the Elder, knowing that's what I'd order, Younger or Elder, no matter, going along with things, as I do, and trusting in Lester Bowie, following his lead, and then I sit at one of the tables just off from the bar since all six chairs at the bar are occupied, which mildly irritates me even though I knew someone would eventually leave, sooner or later, and so I sit there at the table, a high table with a high chair, at the same level of the bar, a conscious decision according to Liz Taylor, sitting at the high table instead of my favorite low table since, like the bar, it too was taken, and so, disgruntled, slightly, miffed, I sit there and read with my pencil at the ready, marking up this passage then that passage, as one does with Arendt, since practically every sentence says something *crucial*, which, when you think of it, is kind of annoying, being something one is essentially forced to do, due to the quality of every damn sentence, being brilliant and all, and so after an half hour or two of doing that, the guys at the bar do indeed stand up to leave, and so one of the guys, seeing me heading anxiously toward the seat, having spied me prior to their exiting, with my anxious eye anxiously on their stools, their high chairs, to be sure, pulls out the seat, or the stool, stool with a back so you can lean back, so you're not slumping there, he pulling out the chair for me and the guy saying, sarcastically, something like *do you want the chair, my friend,* though he said something like *partner* or perhaps something peculiar like *comrade*, though not those words either, me nodding as he pulls out the chair, the high chair, the bar stool with back, like a chair but actually a stool, motioning with his hand and me saying *thanks, my friend*, as if I was John McCain, the Senator, or thanks partner, or comrade, or bud, as if we were friends, making a point of echoing the phrase, whatever it was. Me feeling kind of like a dick, consequently, hovering there, as I, truthfully, was, waiting for the seat, anxiously looking up from my book, as if I could really read it, weighed down as I was by the *felt need* to underline practically every other sentence, not to mention my being ready to pounce, and he pulling out the chair as if to confirm that, he being a kind of dick himself in his making me feel like a dick, even if I was in fact the initial dick, the asshole with his eye on his stool, whatever you want to call it

To the left of me is a woman in her thirties who's sitting next to a large man in a button down shirt and a pair of slacks, one slack per leg, presumably. They've been talking for some time and so I think they must be a couple or at least that they are there together, but she ends up leaving on her own, which is a good sign since it means that a woman was sitting at the bar by herself like the men like to do so much. I'd say "we men" but I'm not sure I'm a *we-man*. After she leaves, the large fellow three seats down from me positions himself in such a way that he is facing me rather than facing straight ahead like one usually does while seated at a bar and I get the feeling that he wants to talk, engage in conversation, but I'm not feeling up to it, in part because he doesn't seem so interesting to me, which I admit may be due to his rather large frame, not that I'm not like totally large, myself, which is, I guess, a way of saying I'm not sure I'd want to strike up a conversation with a fat-fuck like me, either, but also his attire, which is rather formal (suit stripped of tie, collar unbuttoned) for the laid back style of the Stein, though, true, people often come to the Stein dressed in business attire for a power lunch during the weekdays, and some know the Stein only in that capacity, they, as such, not really being Steinians at all, basically not really part of the Stein, the Stein thing, when, that is, the Stein was still *the* place to be, before, that is, the Stein moved house to become a new and improved Stein, eventually becoming, as a result, the Neoliberal Stein, if you will, a cash cow, a generator of quick, dine & dash cash, and then the *cash-in*, on the part of the *owners*, not that the Stein had not long since vanished by the time the sale went down, and not that I blame them, they the owners, the Liz and Dick team, cashing it in having been the plan all along, not that I wouldn't do the same, I mean, wouldn't you do the same if someone offered you that kind of cash, I mean it's not like they didn't work their tails off to achieve that and *you can't tell me you wouldn't have done the same* and so forth, that being the way the conversation usually goes when it comes to conversing about the cash-in phenom, like local brewers selling out to the big breweries or whatever, becoming hippycrits, they, the one-time poets of Eugene, the brewers, that is, *becoming hippycrit*. So, with the big guy to my left positioned in such a way to strike up conversation, I do my best to stay absorbed in my Arendt, which is not difficult to do even though her discussion of Broch is quite complex, the sentences often requiring second readings, actually multiple readings, where you're say sipping on a Pliny, a Pliny the Elder or a Pliny the Younger, or a Blind Pig, depending on what you're handed, handed by Lester Bowie or the Mad Dog, the Mad Dog being even more efficient than the accomplished Lester Bowie at knowing precisely what to pour each customer who sauntered into the Stein, such that the beer was already poured by the time the said customer reached the bar, poured and placed in front of the said customer, the said Steinian, whereas Lester Bowie, not that there's a competition going on here, tended to wait until one was seated at the bar to confirm the drink first, so reading a sentence but not really focused in on it, so you have to read it again, and then something else distracts you, so you read it over, this time paying close attention and because it is an idea that is abstract and difficult to grasp, you end up reading it yet again, finally stepping into the flow of the idea as it unfolds sentence by sentence, maybe underlining a sentence this time or placing a star in the margin, as opposed to a vertical line, or a wavy line in a jazzy like movement. But the large man, who looks like he's from out of town, probably there on business, with a salesman-like look about him, as if stuck in that look by the job, and thus becoming that look, now finding himself alone at the bar, but not wanting to head back to the motel and the teevee set, and so turns on his stool towards me, such that I feel his gaze bearing down on me whilst I remain fixed on Arendt and Broch, thinking of how some of Broch's ideas remind me of some of the things Agamben says in *The Coming Community*, thinking also how reading one book brings other books into play, though I cannot remember now what it was Broch said that brought to mind *The Coming Community*. Finally, the big fellow, who likely, in fact, has some interesting things to say, perhaps we'd end up talking about where he's from or the work he does, and then something deep, finally, the big guy settles his tab and leaves the establishment, right around the time I see a familiar couple enter the Stein, folks I've conversed with before and whose talk I've enjoyed, sometimes, but whose names momentarily escape me, per usual, except that time when Fred, the Fred of the Fred and Ginger duo, their names coming to me now, took issue with Michelle Alexander's thesis, as parlayed to him by me, in *The New Jim Crow*, Fred saying the usual predictable white thing, which I can't remember now except that it's stupid. They, the couple in question, see me and head for the stools vacated by the man and the woman, who, as it turned out, were strangers, even though, at the Stein, they spoke as if they knew each other, the kind of effect the Stein has on people. Then I hear Jack Kerouac, who all along was sitting to the left of the large man and not so large woman, ask the newly arrived couple, Fred and Ginger, who always frequent the Stein together, such that rarely does one encounter Fred without also encountering Ginger, who are about my age, Jack Kerouac asking them how their trip went and so I learn that they too just got back into town, the first part of their trip spent in Knoxville, Tennessee, then moving onto DC and finally Manhattan. There's a stool between us, which I slip over to after the conversation gets going. I explain that I've just come back from vacation in Fort Wayne, Indiana and we, the four of us, have a good chuckle over that, though I explain that in fact we spent the majority of time on these amazing, glacial lakes just north of Fort Wayne, lakes I had no idea were even there even though Sedgwick has told me about them many a time, having spent many a summer there at her friends' cottages, back when she was growing up there in Fort Wayne, a rather dreadful place, in my opinion, but not so for Sedgwick, though, true, she did flee from Fort Wayne to Durango, Colorado, which is where we met. Kind of like Buffalo but without the culture, thought I, though they've done a good job of refurbishing the downtown, Sedgwick pointing out the theater where she saw Peter Gabriel play back in the late 70s, on his first solo tour, Fripp back there in the shadows acting all subtle and all

Look, I'm not saying Fort Wayne can't be as good as any place, as, in the end, you gotta live somewhere, and most times somewhere is as good as anywhere. Yet place is everything, in fact, it's all over you, all your many places being who you are in the end, a placemat full of geography, so to speak, and so, yes, one has to leave such places as Fort Wayne or Fort Collins or Durango, Colorado, because, in the end, that may not be the kind of placemap you want to be

Of course, my two wrong-wing brother-in-laws, one who is still stuck there in the Midwest, Ohio, in his case, which may as well be Indiana, the other in Florida, which is basically like the Midwest with a bit of the Bronx thrown in gone tropical, took their shots or two at our liberal dispositions, me and the Sedgwick (and the Reba, too, she echoing ours, sometimes asking things like "Are we Democrats?" or "Are we going to vote for Obama again?" even though we tell her that she must form her own ideas, rather than simply echoing what we believe—though, of course, we don't mean that), in a drive-by, Willy, Sedgwick's brother, walking diagonally across the room, from the door that leads out to the deck that, in turn, looks out over the lake, the make-shift docks, disassembled in the fall before the snows and freezing temperatures arrive, blurts out:

"WE SHOULD ABOLISH THE DEPARTMENT OF EDUCATION!!!"

and then promptly disappears into the

bathroom for yet another pisser—Willy suffering like me from frequent urination syndrome, though he's worse than me, though, true, also a little older. We're good friends whenever we see each other, when present, when face-to-face, even if afterwards, when we're back to the distance between us, we're likely to think the other fucked up in their thinking, one of us being right and the other being wrong, and vice versa

I'm on the couch and my other brother-in-law Ernie's in the chair that directly faces the television, which is tuned into either Fox News or CNBC, and he has his laptop on his lap, tuned into the markets, his eyes darting back and forth from the television screen to the computer screen, tracking how far gold is going up as the Dow Jones and the S&P and everything else precipitously drops; it's an exciting news week as the stock market crashes in what looks to be a possible repeat of 2008, capped, as it happens, by the collapse of a huge stage at the Indiana State Fair that killed four and injured close to fifty. Later Willy talks to me about how public employees, like myself, being a part-time adjunct at Lane Community College, are paid for by folks like him who work at private sector jobs. You see, he says, what you've got to understand about government jobs is that they are being paid by the taxpayers. This makes people like me entirely dependent on government handouts, handouts that folks like him in the private sector are forced to fork over. I think he's headed toward some argument having to do with self-reliance and such, but instead I respond by saying, so, what you're saying is that I, as a teacher, don't really have a real job, and that I'm like some kind of leach, leaching off the government trough. This he refutes, repeating, nonetheless, what he said before but then the discussion is interrupted by some commotion so that he can't finish his line of reasoning. Neither of us ever quite get around to fleshing out our arguments, in part because we all know by now not to go there, even if each of us actually wishes to go right there, they thinking of what they'll say to us when they see us, and we, the liberals so-called (though I personally prefer "leftists," insofar as *I ain't no milk-toast liberal*), thinking what we'll say to them when we see them (the wrong-wingers), even though, as I said to the right-wing barber before heading off for vacation in Indiana—vacation and Indiana being kind of oxymoronic, to be sure—my response to their provocations or inquiries will simply be "I'm right and you're wrong," end of story, my saying that to the barber basically applying it to him as well, kind of covertly slipping it in, as if he didn't know. The "I'm right and you're wrong" tactic, by the way, is inspired by Bob Marley's "so go to hell if what you're thinking is not right," one of my favorite lines by the man, even if, in the wrong hands, it's *problematic*, as they say

Came in around five to five, having dropped Reba off at soccer practice, early like she likes to be. Took the seat at the end of the bar, happy to see it largely open, maybe a couple others at most sitting at the bar. Made a joke to Lester Bowie about turning the TV to the Republican debate, not really joking since I like to watch that shit. At least I did then. Lester Bowie goes into his own history of having tuned out politics, how expecting government to do something that actually helps people is pointless. I'm thinking Zizek's point about doing nothing if the doing you're doing is just legitimizing the very thing you're trying to change. Better to aim at the Saramago scenario in his novel *Seeing* where everyone basically doesn't vote, thereby creating a constitutional crisis or something and so forth. But how do you know that everyone is going to vote the same way, that is, not vote? What if all the wrong people vote and all the right people don't vote, lacking conviction and all?

A week later or so, Neal Cassady strolls in and takes the chair to my right. He tells me he's not feeling too good, as he tosses back a tall mug of ice water. Too much time in the hot sun, working on cabinets at Oakshire's new Public House, I later piece together. Feeling woozy, the body not yours, yet you totally your body's. Neal Cassady decides to go to the bathroom and wash his face with cold water. I tell Lester Bowie he better check in on the Neal Cassady if he doesn't come back too soon. Joanne K, the nurse two stools down, makes a sarcastic snipe about having to do EPR on someone, yet again. EPR meaning Emergency Preservation and Resuscitation. She's just off from work. We laugh. Neal Cassady comes back, saying he's feeling better, sits down and orders the hummus plate. In between, our having discussed Neal Cassady's supposed ability to time travel while he was off in the bathroom, Lester Bowie tells me about one of his own visions. I'm still stuck on the word "vision" and so don't hear the first part of the story. I stop him because I think I heard the word "dream" in there. *So, wait a second, back up, so your vision was a dream, right?* "Right, it was a dream, you know, a dream vision," he says. Not wanting to dismiss his claim to a "vision" outright, I tell him that the Romans took their dreams very seriously, as well. I learned this from Arendt's book *Men in Dark Times*, which I was reading at the time. I myself do my dreaming at the Stein, which is where I cultivate my visions

At the Stein today ran into Jack Kerouac, who'd been out for the past couple weeks tracking down elk but not managing to kill one. He had been successfully following a herd but somehow lost them, having to go back into town to work a couple days in between. We talked a little about the asshole hunters he encountered on his trip back, after the couple days work, asshole hunters who ended up driving the elk into terrain difficult to navigate, drunk and loaded and trampling all over the place, trigger-happy no doubt, basically harassing the beasts, hounding the beasts, as it were, in essence, total assholes

He talked about running into a cougar on his hunting trip, and I told him about walking up on the Butte, like at the edge of town, and thinking about the fact that someone had seen a cougar just two weeks ago up on the Butte, all of which caused me to feel kind of anxious, cautious, worried, thus walking with heavy stick in hand, as a result, which seriously hampered my walking, my stride, not to mention the whole feel of the walk and the general sense of being a goddamn fool, me with my weapon

Thinking about how you're supposed to look

the beast in the eye and not look away and how you're supposed to hold your hands up high and give off the air of being bigger than the beast, if that is the beast looks like it's going to attack you, and so forth. As if *you're* not the beast, right? You the beast and the cougar just a regular human

Later I crossed some women on the trail and they made me feel like *I* was the cougar, what with me and my *big stick*. (I thought about how I could make a joke about them the two women being the cougars, but in fact they weren't cougars, being younger than that, maybe in their mid-thirties and so just short of being so-called cougars.) I thought about what it must have looked like to see this rather large man huffing and puffing, red in face and puffy, along the trail with some rather oversized supposed walking stick in his hand and so forth, paranoid, as it were, about cougars on the trail. *Seen any cougars around?*

Anyway, Jack Kerouac said he was going to the Further concert in Cuthbert Park, the amphitheater, and so, speaking of concerts, I talked about seeing Dweezle Zappa, Zappa Plays Zappa, on Friday night, who was the lead-in band to Return to Forever, which featured a lot of the original band: Chic Corea, or course, Stanley Clarke, of course, Billy Cobham, of course, but also Jean Luc Ponty. I went to the Stein hoping to find someone who had been there for that, having myself gone alone, and, as it happens, Corso, one of the cooks, and a good Steinian friend, as it were, a soft spoken basically great guy, who, after Jack Kerouac departed, came up, having overheard our conversation, or part of it, the kitchen being out in the open and so basically a part of the bar itself, came up to talk about the concert, having been there himself, to the concert, that is, and so we talking about it for a time, polishing off our beers and then departing, sensibly, knowing how easy it would be to have ordered another wee one for the road, as my Scottish friend Eve used to say over G&T's in the pubs in London. Okay, here's what happened between Eve and me, I say to Corso, as if he cared, Eve and I, once being such close friends, and just like that we never speak or see each other again, but Corso had to leave the Stein, and wasn't paying attention anyway, so this story is left untold, but yet stories, with their narrative arc and all, are not what *Noch Ein* is all about

At the Return to Forever/Dweezle Plays Zappa concert, having imbibed in my share of brews before the show, prepping myself for the experience, and so having to take yet another pisser, this one in the middle of a Zappa tune, I raced up the aisle toward the bathroom and, failing to see the step ahead of me, tripped and fell hard to the floor right in front of everyone, this the sort of action usually left out of *Noch Ein*

It was planned even though I had not previously planned it, knowing only that I'd do it, but not really planned out, but knowing deep down that I'd be doing it. That is, going to the Stein after work, regardless the hour. As it turned out, after announcing to Debbie Harry, the bartender, that it was my birthday—as one does at my age, I didn't mention my age, naturally—going there expecting a free first drink—even at my age, still thinking that way—everyone working there buying my next drink, after the initial free one, making me not only semi-drunk, since I didn't take everyone up on the offer, but more importantly feeling like I was loved, to be honest—but then liquor often makes one feel that way (or the opposite, for some). But loved in the community sense of love. Not that we are *in love* with each other, or that we really actually *love each other*, which, in any case, tends to be something we feel largely upon the loved one's departure and not so much when we're there around each other on a daily basis, year after year, decade after decade, in the fluidity of a long-term love construction, not so much that kind of love then but love in the sense that we are socially aware, individually of each other, our presence, side by side beside each other, engaged on a fairly regular basis, in however a manner, and hence we care and value, if not love, each other. And some of us, most if not all of us in some way or another, need that love to live, which is why we come to a place like the Stein, at least for a stretch, before, that is, our little utopia gets neoliberalized, as the plot has it, and hence destroys everything that it once was, all that potential embodied there in that no-place that was once a yes-place, though, in hindsight, I begrudgingly came to realize that the Stein had been a neoliberal gig all along, part of the ten-year plan, as it happens, and that it was just me projecting my commie junk onto the neoliberal slate the Stein had always-already been, begrudgingly coming to realize that I was the only one, the only Steinian, who had the communist horizon in mind, however much I tried to talk it into being, so, this social love wherein the bartenders and the cooks and the customers and even the owners, we're all like one, all of us existing there for each other, as opposed to extracting something from each other, but which, actually, in the end, turned out to be something privately theirs alone, they the owners, however generous personally the Liz and Dick team may have seemed to have been, in the end, busy extracting, the Stein being after all a privatized space, the Stein a mere stepping stone for something bigger, the future theirs alone yet somehow ours too insofar as undergirding their investment, the risk-taking and the countless hours put in to make it work, as the argument goes, it was us, we in our now snuffed-out we-subjectivity, workers as well customers, the Steinians who created the cultural capital that made the Stein what it was, this line of thought, by the way, coming courtesy of Marxist geographer David Harvey's book *Rebel Cities*, a book many times present at the bar in the Stein, cover up or cover down, sending out its commie vibe, Harvey applying it to cities like San Francisco, now gutted of those who made the city what it was, *wouldn't you do the same?* goes the logic of the investor class, this being the usual reaction to my communist blather, my siccing Harvey on the Stein, his book there in the room, cover up or cover down, falling, to be sure, on deaf ears, though surreptitiously a-vibbing, such that, after a brief consideration, even the likes of Bill Burroughs ends up finally saying it, *well, wouldn't you do the same* etc, i.e. take the money and run, sell the thing and take a cruise, a cruise that lasts a lifetime, I mean wouldn't you be a fool to turn down that kind of money, this being the logic of those like Bill Burroughs, a former real estate agent and before that engineer, after all those years of hard work, hard work you alone endured, carrying the burden, yours alone, the risk etc, speaking here of the Dick and Liz team but also B Burroughs, unlike those we employed or those we served who took no risk at all, worked hard, yes, but didn't plan ahead, lived for the moment and all, nothing invested on their part, who, on their part, provided no jobs, depending on others to create jobs for them, and so, on and on, goes the logic of entrepreneurs and the investor class—*and you've got the Lars Larson Show*

I used to think that the brewers were the poets of Eugene. As I used to proclaim, "The poets in Eugene are the brewers!" Frankly, I don't know what's up with the poets in Eugene, the poets who write poetry, that is, I used to say, where they gather, what they do, whether they loaf or not. Hanging out at the bars, particularly the Stein, but also pubs like 16 Tons or Falling Sky or The Horsehead, bars being where you're going to run into the poets but where are they? Finding none there—save Ty Connor, the bartender at The Horsehead, he being the exception—I came to realize that the poets of Eugene are the brewers, not the poets, the actual poets being nowhere in sight, from what I can tell, me being still a stranger to this town at the time and so wondering where all the poets were in Eugene, they not being in the bars. Perhaps it was due to their healthy ways, I thought, these poets, and thus, like the fitness freaks, generally absented from bars, speaking here of the poets in Eugene and not the brewers who are the real poets of Eugene. As such, they the poets, speaking here not of the brewers who are the real poets of Eugene but of the poets who write poetry, they, having once been alcoholics, say, these so-called poets, are now clean and hence healthy, and so out of sight, I thought, they and their bodies, these poets who are *out to lunch,* that is to say, not in the bars in Eugene where, on the other hand, the real poets of Eugene, they being the brewers, could be found

Loafing at the Stein is not only about drinking beer, as it were, it's also about hanging or loafing with the poets, the brewers, that is to say, the makers, at least before they went neo-liberal and sold their souls, totally erasing the warm rays of the communist horizon shining in our very mists, a horizon, it turns out, only I could see, or only I *wanted* to see. Whether you talk to them or not, no matter, I used to say. Just being there around the poetry is enough, I used to say. It's about living it, the poetry and its making, which means hanging out in bars (or, okay, cafes), I used to say, and so studying it, in effect, "it" being the living of it, for attention is the natural prayer of the soul, as someone once put it. "Let's google it and find out," my interlocutor Bill Burroughs at the Stein says, eager to get out his new device and derail the conversation

"I think of Male-branche's maxim, 'Attentiveness is the natural prayer of the soul.' This maxim, beloved by Simone Weil and Paul Celan, quoted by Walter Benjamin in his magisterial essay on Franz Kafka, can stand as a writer's credo."
http://www.nytimes.com/books/first/h/hirsch-poem.html

("Soul," "natural," whatever.)

Anyway, in regards to beer, this *attentiveness* that the Male-branche subjectivity speaks of means talking about the beer itself as one is drinking the beer itself. Like meta-fiction, drinking beer means talking beer as one is drinking beer. Talking hops, etcetera. Talking abv's and ibu's, etcetera. Maybe you throw in some this and some that in there. Maybe you brew in bourbon kegs. IPAs this, Reds that. Pale Ale and Sours. Throw in some lavender, say. Or throw in some vanilla bean. The latter not for me. Some espresso in that Stout, thick and creamy. And so forth. This one with glacier water, that one with roasted barley. Cardamom and orange peel. Some raspy berries and what not. One talks about many things at the Stein but the common language is beer talk. There's a small, old fashion (read: non-flat screen) teevee set in the corner that most everyone ignores, and which mostly is turned off, which, for me, is the best way to watch teevee. True, it's mostly sports that's on the teevee when it's unfortunately turned on but at the Stein beer trumps sports any day when it comes to conversing, conversing between men, men mostly, mostly white men, that is—a flaw, to be sure, not just in the Stein itself but also, as a consequence, in *Noch Ein at the Stein.* Though sometimes there are women at the bar, which is nice, mostly white women, that is. I myself like to see women sitting alone at the Stein, preferably at the bar, not so that I can try to seduce them or shimmy up next to them, but so that I feel less guilty about hanging out with just men, conversing primarily with men, though on occasion, thankfully, some women sometimes too. Just so you don't feel like it's a men's club, which it is, the brewing biz too mostly a male thing, though there are those like Hilda Dolittle, for example, who once was at Oakshire and then at Ninkasi but who was originally at the Stein. Hopefully, that's a sign of change. For women, after all, were the original brewers, at least back in the Middle Ages, before the alehouses and taverns and inns entered the scene, according to the book I'm reading. They, the women, would brew it in order to make some extra cash, selling it here and there, to travelers, vagabonds, and to the locals. Brewing up a batch, now and then, when they had the time, time and materials, getting drunk on occasion, as well, as I am imagining it, projecting such things as I do like the aforementioned communist horizon, which will be, I say to Bill Burroughs, what one critic calls "fully automated luxury communism," our heaven having beer, I say to Bill Burroughs, heaven being here, in the future-anterior sense, I said to Bill Burroughs, saying it and so making it so—*make it so*

I told Lizzy that the Stein reminds me of French's in London. No TV set, no music (though, as noted, the Stein unfortunately does have a teevee—it's an American* establishment, after all, but it's mostly turned off, and, yes, the Stein does play music, but mostly good music; ideally, of course, there'd be no music), bright lighting, so you can read if you wish, the sound of conversations meshing, the mash of talk. That's all. Just that. The talk going nowhere, of course, just like *Noch Ein at the Stein*, which, if you haven't figured it out by now, dear reader, is going nowhere, no where but here, on this stool. Mission Statement: *Noch Ein* is content with just sitting on its stool, going nowhere, fast or slow, what have you. Plus the drinks, of course, drink being a key component of good conversation, though, not a necessity. Over there, at French's (or The French House), it'd be wine, Pernod, and half-pints of lager, regardless of gender. Since it was a French establishment, there was nothing emasculating about the half-pints, normally meant for the women in the regular, English pubs, drinking full pints being very unladylike, according to the Brits. At least it was that way back when I lived there, back in the mid-to-late 80s, back in the day, as they say (though the days were hardly *back in the day* back then due to Thatcher in England and Reagan in the USA, the latter two being against the day). French's was almost always packed, packed with people talking and rubbing shoulders with their *shoulder buddy*, the latter term picked up in a seminar on equity I attended the other day: "Now turn to your shoulder-buddy and tell them about a memory of no import but that says something about who you really are"

> "Actors, writers, artists and wits rub shoulders with royalty, bohemians and the film world in this, the most iconic of Soho watering holes. A fabulous and entertaining spot to raise a glass in London, the French House truly deserves its reputation as the best known pub in the world's naughtiest square mile. Its no music, no machines, no television and no mobile phones rule makes it a haven for conversationalists and a firm favourite among some of the best known names in showbusiness."
> http://www.frenchhousesoho.com

The painter Frances Bacon used to hang out there, apparently, as well as other luminaries. Not that we, the unfamous, care about such humans, or that we let their illustriousness get to us, we being basically absent of luminaryness, though we too become illuminated from time to time, especially when set foot in the likes of the Stein, thanks in part to the owners Dick and Liz, but really thanks to the cultural capital of those under their employ and the Steinians they attracted, a cultural capital eventually demolished, as noted, once the Stein went neoliberal and moved house to the Neo-Stein, though lately, against all odds, a proximation of the communist horizon has once again begun to emerge in the form of the Neo-Stein's town hall like vibe, at least I like to pretend it does, still frequenting the Stein, as I do, despite the fact that the Neo-Stein is nothing but a cash cow now and hence a dead end for those in its employ, just like every other establishment in this town, once a town of hippies but now just the usual hippycrits abounding

Speaking of Bacon, being around painters is like being around poets, not that you necessarily want to talk to them, given that they won't really talk to you, these painters, unlike the poets who love to talk, save the solitary types, those into solitude, into getting away in order to write, they the clean ones, formerly addicts or alcoholics but now into yoga or something, earnest workshop types all wrapped up in their solitude, their retreats with their prompts, as if the writing doesn't happen down here *in the midst of the action*, as the Good Doctor once said, in the streets or on a choice stool at the Stein, speaking here of William Carlos Williams, of course, the poet from Rutherford, New Jersey. Still, being in the company of artists, even poets, is where one prefers to be, nevertheless. It is at places like the Stein, which is the only place I venture, save occasionally the Highlands, which is nothing like the Stein, due to the former's proximity—I can walk home from the Highlands, living as we do in the South Hills, though I rarely do, preferring the car and the loud music, lately Deerhoof, but then suddenly I'm over Deerhoof, for the moment, waiting for the next fix, maybe Tom Zé's *Estudando a Bossa (Nordeste Plaza)*, for example, or, say, Thundercat's *Drunk*. It was at places like the old Stein that you could run into these Eugene poets, these master brewers. Sometimes I'd see Jim Morrison there at the Stein, Jim being one of the most famous poets in town, though some say, yes, but is he really a poet, now that he's turned hippycrit? They saying that not me, just saying. He'd become a star and people often behaved around him like he was a star. Me included. Not that that's his fault. Though, true, he allowed himself to become rich, expanding the brewery, as they did, exponentially, so that now you can find them on the East Coast, but that was in the plan all along, apparently. I'd see Jim Morrison's sidekick, Robby Krieger, the mastermind behind master-brewer Morrison, around town here and there, early on in the game, on occasion, before they grew and hired staff to do the deliveries, at Jiffy Market, for example, one of the other great hangouts in Eugene, while it still existed, the owners deciding to retire, the two brothers who inherited it from their father, who took turns at the cash register, also great conversationalists. It was a place where one might have run into some poets, though they were more of the wine sort, earnestly into wine kind of poets, even if Jiffy Market had a handful of local beers on tap and in the refrigerators, the racks. Of course, there were the other famous poets of Eugene, whose names escape me, due perhaps to their failure or their success, that is to say their commercialization, the legends before folks like Jim Morrison entered the fray, he and the other up-and-coming brewers popping up willy-nilly here and there in Eugene, one after the other, and then there were the *aspiring* poets, those who home-brewed, maybe just passing it around among friends, or publishing their works at the monthly gatherings, the self-published poets, brewing beer because they loved to make it, the process and all, the learning curve, actually losing money in the process, just like poets writing for nothing, exemplary of the new economy to come

Talking about beer at the Stein invariably leads to talking about food. Much of this has to do with my getting to know the cooking staff, thanks to the kitchen being open to view, and the fact that the kitchen staff sometimes stay on after work for a pint or two, sitting at the bar or at a table together, talking with the customers, some of whom have become friends. (Later, at the Neo-Stein, they were forbidden from sitting at the bar after work, confined to the tables or their own private loft that partially overlooked the bar, tucked away from the public sphere, out of sight, like the new kitchen.) That the kitchen is part of the bar just as the bar is part of the restaurant just as the bar and the restaurant and the kitchen are part of the *bottle shop*. We are in fact concerned that when they move house they'll lose the communist (my word for it) quality of the establishment as it exists now. Though true, with it, we'll also lose that Steinian smell, the stink that lingers on in the clothes, I'm told. Me, I can't smell it, and neither can Sedgwick, she not aware of it when I tell her about it. But the wives of some of the guys can. *Ah, been at the Stein, huh?* Later, when I'm at Henry David's house down the street,

I tell Henry David that, unlike his wife, Sedgwick can't smell it, which I find odd since Sedgwick smells things I can't smell all the time. This then leads to a discussion about whether women, in general, can smell better than men. I say, maybe there's something specific about women in general, generally speaking, that enables them to smell better than men. Henry David, my scientist neighbor and frequenter at the Stein, says that there's likely nothing genetic about it but that, yes, it seems women are more attuned to senses like smell. And what about pain, I ask my neighbor Henry David the scientist, Sedgwick claims that she has a strong tolerance for pain, I ask her how do you know and she says she's always been that way, but Henry David is not so sure that this is a universal trait for female humans though he says it likely has something to do with giving birth. "Perhaps smell's like that, too, linked to child bearing," I say. Given that Henry David is a fish scientist, this then leads to the oft asked question about whether fish can feel pain, this a question asked by those who don't fish, don't fish because they think fish feel pain and so how would you feel if someone hooked you in the mouth, tricked you into eating a delicious meal that turned out to come with a hook? Oregon being of course a destination spot for fishing, especially the beautiful McKenzie River. Henry David confirms that fish do indeed feel pain, which doesn't stop him from fishing, he owning a drift boat, plus all the other fishing equipment, being a gadget guy and so having all the equipment. After all, Henry David, being a fish scientist, is killing fish all the time, in the name of research, researching DNA and all. I finish this line of talk by returning to the smell question and whether Henry David's wife can always tell when he's been at the Stein because the Stein stinks, apparently, or rather, the Stein has a distinct smell, a musky kind of sour smell, and I say that even though Sedgwick can't smell the Stein on me when I return home after a couple of pints—and it's always a "couple of pints," rather than, say, four pints or more commonly three and a half, the half being my way of keeping it down under four, in an attempt to persuade myself that I'm not really drinking that much such that when I tell Sedgwick I'm heading to the Stein for a "couple of pints," that's more or less accurate, even if I invariably have to add another "wee one" or two for the road—I say to Henry David that, even though Sedgwick smells everything but for some mysterious reason not the Stein, that it doesn't matter since Sedgwick always knows where I am, to which Henry David responds, "Perhaps that's why she doesn't smell the Stein on you, because she doesn't have to, she knows where you are." (Husbands and wives always keeping track of each other being what marriage is all about.) Of course, Henry David's wife Pam always knows where he is because those two are always texting each other back and forth constantly throughout the day, such that it's hard to carry on a conversation with Henry David, he always distracted, distracted and sighing, a heavy sigher, if not by an actual text then by the anticipation of an actual text, which he doesn't seem to have a problem with, in fact, it's like he's enjoying the fact that an incoming text is about to come his way. I've told him more than once I find it quite annoying, but Henry David's a gadget guy so there's no convincing him. As such, our conversations tend to be fragmentary, marked by stops and starts, which inevitably leads to a splintering of the syntax, a kind of schizophrenic dialogue that meanders this way and that willy nilly, full of pot holes and bad grammar, sentence fragments, comma splices and run-ons, mixed constructions, non-sequiturs and such

That the cooks will disappear from view, that's our concern with the new Stein in the making. These cooks, some of whom have become friends, will hence disappear. Back there working away, alienated from their labor and from the public at large, food magically appearing in the window, window to table, fork or spoon or hand to mouth, magically, out of sight, alienated, neoliberal food. No longer seeing the process, the labor behind the food. That's a concern. But, frankly, the Stein is becoming too packed to visit these days, especially when school's in session, thanks to the graduate students and all, my post-doc fish-geek friends, for example, sometimes suddenly there, there alone at their table, curling in on themselves with their science talk, they with their science talk and fish-geek jokes and all, hilarious stuff about cichlids and such, Zebra fish, for example, jokes of that sort. I too was once gladly associated with academe, and a college kid once myself, not to mention a gradual student, and in fact often long for those days when we'd hang out in the pubs and so forth, having the conversations, going on about poetry, like they go on about beer here, hops this hops that. For us, back there in

Buffalo, it was Zuk this and Rez that and Stein this and Niedecker that, Emily Dickinson and Susan Howe this that and that this, in our neck of the woods back there in Buffalo, back then in the hey-day of the Poetics Program. But, frankly, the way in which the university crowd has overtaken the place has made it unappealing to we, the loyalists, the original Steinians, that is to say. It's become as such a matter of timing, of locating that crease in the day, between one shift of people going out and the next shift of people coming in, entering or leaving the Stein. A brief lull, the sudden quiet, maybe even a lapse in the music, with but a mere single soul parked at end of the bar, the other five stools open, a kind of utopia opening up before your very eyes, there in the no-place an empty stool, room enough for you and a friend or two to wander in out of nowhere and saddle up to the bar, that heavenly spot of time, there at the old Stein, when the communist horizon was still in view, that is, still in view for me, I being for sure the only Steinian thinking these commie things, though the others, Bill Burroughs, for example, and Charlie Olson, for example, hearing plenty of it from me, me, for example, bending Bill Burroughs ear about it, he being interested enough to hear about it, debate it with me, my bending his ear and he bending mine and hearing about it, but, having once been an engineer and later a real estate agent, naturally rejecting it, me telling him I too don't really believe it, though, true, I do long for it, kind of, this being an instance of communist longing, longing for something whose contents we have no idea of: "'we wake in the morning, and we go out in the garden, till the ground, and in the afternoon we engage in criticism'" (Marx qtd. in Moten)

Last night at the Stein was one of the best evenings in quite a while, thanks in good part to Brother Anthony, who is an excellent *shoulder buddy,* excellent interlocutor, that is to say, such that conversation sometimes pools up in his mouth in the form of saliva, this being due to his cerebral palsy. I used to have a friend, a friend in his fifties who gave up his business career to go back to grad school and study poetry, who'd produce these white balls of crud in the corners of his mouth when he talked. That definitely grossed some people out and it's true, sometimes I'd want to tell him that he had a white ball of waxen-like spittle or crud lurking there in the corner of his mouth again and that he might want to wipe that away. As if it was his fault. That is how people would react to it, myself often included. As in, *Gross, dude, wipe that crud away,* the human body being gross and all. But it wasn't just Brother Anthony, because Bill Burroughs was there as well, having shown up soon after I happened to snare the seat next to Brother Anthony. Brother Anthony spotted me as I entered the Stein and hailed after me, indicating that there was an empty seat right next to him and so

I walked over to the stool, one of six, and took it, sitting down next to him. We had had excellent conversation the last time we saw each other, but then, being an accomplished conversationalist, we always had excellent conversation. I told him that I was happy to see him because I had something in mind I wanted to talk about or talk through with someone, someone who was capable of handling the thought and developing it together, and that he was perfectly suited to it being a most excellent interlocutor. I told him how good it was to be able to converse with such an accomplished conversationalist, the kind that can follow the conversation wherever it takes us, each being capable and, moreover, willing to follow the other's leads, the subject matter and so forth, sometimes familiar with it and other times not and so explaining at first, and not worrying about getting to any specific point or resolving any matter, he doing that with me and me doing that with him, back and forth, back and forth, and so forth. He chalked it up to providence; such meetings aren't accidental, he believed, his being a Catholic. Although I generally don't tend to think that way, I did enjoy the thought, a thought

I could languish in without believing it. Brother Anthony being a Catholic and so believing in such things as providence and me being able to enjoy the luxury, the pleasure, the permission to imagine such a thing as providence, without having to believe it. Though there may be such a thing as providence without purpose, I entertained in a side bar in my mind whilst Brother Anthony was going on about providence. Like in that case with that woman in Berlin. West Berlin, when the Wall was still up, who, later, when I had moved to London, I kept running into everywhere, though we were strangers and in fact I had never talked to her and in fact only seen her that one time in Berlin, her visage obviously making a strong impression on me and that, while seated on a bus, I heard her saying goodbye to a friend in English through the bus door before it sneezed shut, having never talked to her, until that one time much later, when it seemed downright uncanny and so I had to say something, having, in fact, run randomly into her walking down the street in Tufnell Park, where I lived in London, and then later at the movie theatre, the Lumière, where I saw *Blue Velvet*, not just once but twice, and then, uncannily, at a travel agency, when I was booking a flight to Berlin and over-hearing her travel plans, discovered that she too was booking a flight to Berlin, and so realizing then and there that indeed it *was* her, the very same blond-haired Irish or was it Scottish woman I had heard speaking English to a friend as she stepped alone onto the bus I was on in West Berlin, which is why when, later, at a Carol Ann Duffy poetry reading, she showed up with a friend, and after telling this story to my friend Wendy who was there with me for the reading and who encouraged me to introduce myself to her and tell her this story, I eventually did finally talk to her, thanks to Wendy, given that it was a poetry reading and that I knew Carol Ann personally, thanks to her publishing my poetry in *Ambit*, the poetry journal where she served as an editor, which, as it happens, turned out to be the last time I saw the woman in question, though not because I had said anything offensive, just recounted the whole story, which, true, must have seemed rather creepy, as if I was stalking her or something, my deciding because of that not to ask her for her number. People always feel cheated when I tell them this story but for me it's just this way people have of crossing paths at distinct times that makes it seem like something else is going on out there when in fact nothing's going on in or out there and even if it was so what? Must we accept the invitation? I hadn't seen Bill Burroughs for quite a while and when Bill Burroughs tapped me on the shoulder with a welcome to me and Brother Anthony, I could tell he wanted to join in but that was impossible because the only seat available was at the end of the bar, which is where Bill Burroughs decided to sit. He came over after a little while with a question for us, wondering how to spell hegemony. I told him I thought it was h e g e m o n y, and Brother Anthony confirmed it. Bill Burroughs then offered up his definition, which I cannot currently recall but I remember that I was pretty sure he was wrong. So I told him to get out his toy—his smart phone—and look it up, teasing him about his newly acquired gadget, me being kind of an asshole about it, I admit, not having such a gadget myself yet, just an old and embarrassing flip-phone. It's not that Bill Burroughs, like Henry David, was a gadget

129

person, except that he was, only that he had just recently bought it and so was enjoying the opportunity to get it out and use it, for why buy something and then not use it? It made sense that he'd get sucked into his new gadget as he had been an engineer at one point in his long life, into air conditioning, big buildings and so forth. Bill Burroughs telling me about the time he was flown out to the Hong Kong airport to fix the air conditioning, only to find that it was merely a matter of flipping the switch. Nevertheless, Bill Burroughs was hailed as a genius and enjoyed the rest of his time in Hong Kong, lounging about no doubt, on company time, naturally. Not too long after his question about hegemony, George Harrison came in, shouldering up beside me to my right on the stool just recently vacated. On my left was Brother Anthony and on my right was George Harrison, with Bill Burroughs curling in on his gadget, absorbing information off in the near distance. Brother Anthony, who is a lawyer, is something of a conservative. George Harrison on the other hand is no doubt a liberal, being as he is a musician (guitarist), he was stopping by for a quick pint before rehearsal with his band.

Initially the band was a John Lennon tribute band, which they got together for the 30th anniversary of John Lennon's death last year, but now they are working more on their own material. But before George Harrison showed, Brother Anthony and I had gone from talking about TV shows, to film. He had just seen the new film *Tinker, Tailor, Soldier, Spy* and I asked him whether it was good or not because I was inclined to go see it, enjoying those old Cold War spy movies just as he, Brother Anthony, did. As it turns out, it doesn't matter now since the movie theaters at the mall aren't showing it anymore. Sedgwick said that's why you just gotta go see the film right away when it comes out because it'll be gone in a week in most cases, unlike in days of old, like say the 70s, when a film like *Taxi Driver* would stick around for a good month, this being before Spielberg came along and totally destroyed the movie industry with anti-science schlock like *E.T.* and racist shit like *Indiana Jones*, the perfect way to issue in the Reagan. Then I asked Brother Anthony whether he had seen *The Girl with the Dragon Tattoo* and he said not the most recent one but that he had seen the Swedish version, which he had to walk out on due to the disturbing rape scene—not that he didn't appreciate the film itself, I presumed. He said he was hesitant to go see the new English version because of that and I told him it wasn't that bad, as if a rape scene can be just mildly bad. Then I told him about the rape scene in Gaspar Noé's film *Irreversible*, which is about as extreme as you can get it seems to me and how the rape scene in the recent version of *The Girl with the Dragon Tattoo* is mild in comparison, which, again, struck me as rather disturbing when I said it, that a rape scene could be "rather mild." We then talked about whether the violence was justified in Gaspar Noé's film *Irreversible* and so I had to tell him about the narrative structure of the film, because that's crucial to the film's meaning and to whether the violence was justified or simply gratuitous, there for shock value alone, to uphold the director's reputation as a bad boy, some kind of European David Lynch, apparently, *Eurolynch*. The fact that the narrative runs backwards, starting with the ending and ending with the beginning and that since the film started with a gruesome murder scene that then led back to a gruesome and possibly fatal rape scene that then wound its way back to a beautiful morning in bed scene, with the two protagonists making sweet love and so forth, that changes how you see the violence. We then talked about how to interpret the backwards narrative, chronologically speaking, and the fact that the movie has a happy ending, as a consequence of this reversal of events, but only after we've been presented with the sheer, ugly brutality of the world, its rapes its murders its cruelty its viciousness: was it meant to be interpreted as a sign of optimism, a reminder that there is love in this world and there is beauty in this world despite the ugliness everywhere abounding, or was it a sign of pessimism or even cynicism, that it is impossible to see this love in this world and this beauty in this world given our knowledge of the rape and murder in this world that seems to be everywhere abounding these days in this world, these days of screens, of screen-time. This is when George Harrison showed up, parking right next to me in the recently vacated seat, with Brother Anthony to my left as I have said already. We spoke about music for a while because as I said George

Harrison is a musician and also because that's how I had initially started the conversation with Brother Anthony, mentioning to both of them now that I had just been to the library where I picked up a compact disc (cd) by Captain Beefheart, as well as Frank Zappa, Led Zeppelin III, and two cds by Wilco, who I didn't know that well. But it was Captain Beefheart I wanted to talk about because that's what I was listening to in the car stereo before arriving at the Stein. I told Brother Anthony, who's about my age, in his early fifties and so would probably know a little about Captain Beefheart, even though I myself am just getting to know Captain Beefheart's music. But I was pleased to run into Brother Anthony because I knew I could talk to him about Captain Beefheart and how radical and innovative the music still seems, though admittedly the recording is not the best on the particular cd I've checked out. Who else, I said, do you know who would dare to title a song "Dachau Blues"? So I mentioned Captain Beefheart to George Harrison, who himself is in his early sixties, but it wasn't until I mentioned Wilco that George Harrison perked up, discussing how they were clearly influenced by the Beetles and also how accomplished the band is insofar as their musicianship is always in the interest of the song and not their egos. George Harrison then switched topics to the good news about their trailer park up the McKenzie river in the town of Vida and how they as a community collectively just bought the trailer park. We all later agreed that someone needs to write about this, I mean, like a journalist for the *Register-Guard* or the *Eugene Weekly*. My interest in Captain Beefheart had in part come from learning that Captain Beefheart's guitarist lives in town and in fact teaches at the local community college just like I do, which made me think that I must bone up on the Captain Beefheart so that if I somehow end up meeting this Captain Beefheart guitarist, being on a kind of quest to meet the guitarist, Zoot Horn Rollo, that is, that I'll be able to actually say that I'm familiar with his work, and move from that into conversation, but all George Harrison wanted to talk about, after telling his captivating and inspiring story about his now collective-owned trailer park up in Vida, was the band Wilco who I thought, after a number of listenings, were just so-so, even though I also like *just so-so* music, everything doesn't always have to be brilliant in one's life after all and, indeed, there are times when one gets tired of genius

And indeed I finally did meet the guitarist in question, Zoot Horn Rollo, at the Neo-Stein. Apparently, Zoot Horn Rollo had been hanging out at the Stein all along, the Neo-Stein, that is, not knowing yet whether he also hung out at the OG-Stein. "You've seen him," said Charlie Olson to me while seated at what he and Wilber christened "Asshole Corner," a moniker I rejected outright, preferring "Corner Club," in honor of Milton Nascimento and Lô Borges's classic album *Clube da Esquina*, which I picked up in Brasil back in the late seventies when I lived there for a little bit, but they, those who hang out at *Asshole Corner*, knew not of *Clube da Esquina*, nor Milton Nascimento, nor for that matter the much more obscure Lô Borges, so *Asshole Corner* won the day, much to my chagrin, not that I don't forgive them, my Corner Club friends. "You've seen him," Charlie Olson saying, "he usually sits alone at the bar with his laptop, working away on something. He's a nice guy, you two would get along," and so forth, Charlie Olson saying. And so, one day, on *that* day, when on my quest to meet Captain Beefheart guitarist Zoot Horn Rollo, I actually met Zoot Horn Rollo, at the Neo-Stein no less, an establishment I obviously still frequent, if not *always*, despite the Stein's hippycritical turn and the subsequent erasure of my communist horizon delusion, figuring the Neo-Stein wasn't that bad after all, admitting defeat, in effect, and that my commie horizon was just a fantasy, all along, no matter how much I still continue to live as if such a horizon has already been achieved, choosing, as I do, to live in the "*futur antérieur,*" wherein one lives life according to what one hopes for in the future as if it was actually here, here right now in the present as we speak, on that day, Charlie Olson noticed him seated across the bar from us at the Neo-Stein and so said to me, "That's him over there," gesturing with his head, a *head nod*, instead of pointing, which is impolite, but then Captain Beefheart guitarist Zoot Horn Rollo by that time had in turn noticed Charlie Olson, Rollo recognizing Olson because they had conversed numerous times before, "That's him over there," said Charlie Olson, informing me that, although Zoot Horn Rollo is a humble soul, he was nonetheless an accomplished conversationalist, being one that listens well, as well, being an accomplished conversationalist meaning that one is also an accomplished listener, needless to say, but not the kind of listener who lets his or her interlocutor run roughshod over the conversation, dominating it and so forth, talking practically the whole time, mostly stuff about himself, and never bothering to stop to invite his or her interlocutor to talk him or herself, whether talking about him or herself or not. Anyway, Zoot Horn Rollo, seeing Charlie Olson and me looking over at him from across the bar, quite probably figuring out that Charlie Olson was telling me that that was Zoot Horn Rollo, legendary guitarist for Captain Beefheart, he, Zoot Horn Rollo returned our gaze, and so Charlie Olson, realizing that Zoot Horn Rollo had noticed us talking about him and that he was now gazing back at us, waved at Zoot Horn Rollo, and so he waved back at us, which is when I waved at him too, waved and smiled, as if we already knew each other

Not too long after this and a couple subsequent encounters with the Rollo in question, Sedgwick and I were dining at her favorite establishment Turtles, *her* Stein—though she was not quite as obsessed with hers as I was mine, save Turtle's killer salads and Bloody Marys (now a thing of the past due to Covid)—and having heard me rambling on about the famous guitarist ad nauseam, and how I had met the maestro just last week, we came across the man himself seated at the bar with his back to us and so, my having spotted him, thinking that it was actually him seated there, pointed him out to Sedgwick, saying, "I think that's Zoot Horn Rollo right there," and he then standing up to leave, as it happens, turned around to see the both of us seated there at our table, nursing our beverages, which caused him to do a double take, he looking at Sedgwick and then looking at me and then looking at me again and then looking at Sedgwick again, which is when the three of us realized that we had been connected for quite some time but without knowing it, the two of them way before me, Sedgwick having been shoulder-buddies with the Zoot all along, for a number of years now, but without knowing that he was legendary guitarist Zoot Horn Rollo, even though, yes, she knew he played guitar, he, a musician seemingly no different than the other Turtle regular/ shoulder-buddy who played violin for the Eugene Symphony, but Sedgwick not knowing the rest of Rollo's story, he never revealing it, apparently, his being a member of Beefheart's "Magic Band" on what's considered their "magnum opus," *Trout Mask Replica*, "produced" by Beefheart's (Don Van Vliet's) high school friend Frank Zappa—though, Zappa basically just sat around during the recording, according to ZHR, due perhaps to the fact that the band had rehearsed the material for a good year, however chaotic it initially sounds—a work now "considered to be a groundbreaking avant-rock masterpiece," a favorite of other luminaries like David Lynch, John Lydon, and Matt Groening, but yet, here he was, the legend himself, a status he clearly meant to evade, side by side humbly beside us, just living life like the rest of us non-luminaries

Henry David said he saw Bill Burroughs at Falling Sky the other day. Burroughs was eating lunch or dinner there with his two lesbian friends. They're a couple and since they're both women, that makes them *lesbians*. Right? I happen to know the two women in question, they're both either in their late fifties or their early sixties, but, being bad with names, I forgot their names. I shall call after them as Gertrude and Alice; this by way of honoring them. I had sat at their table once at the Stein thanks to Bill Burroughs, who called after me, seeing that there wasn't a seat at the bar, which I'd otherwise have taken, of course. I had met them already, however, somewhere. "Somewhere, somewhere, somewhere, somewhere," this a quote from a Stereolab song—the soundtrack for this section of the movie version of *Noch Ein*. But it was likely at the Stein, at the bar maybe most likely, that I had originally met them, such a nice couple. We ended up discussing art, with me explaining why representation, especially when it comes to beauty, is so problematic today. It was like I was giving a mini-lecture of an overview on art history to Gertrude, Alice, and Bill Burroughs, of all people, not that I meant to lecture on about it. It had something to do with my poetry, they having inquired about that, what kind of stuff I write and me telling them about the difficulty I had with all this beauty when we first moved to Eugene, living in the woods and all, the deer and the turkeys and the said critters, the crows, the jays, raptors, bats at night, chickadees, woodpeckers, not to mention the spiders and their spider webs, and how I didn't want to write the typical nature poetry, painting pictures of nature scenes when you could just take a daguerrotype of them instead, but nonetheless felt compelled by the nature to write the nature somehow, that being my dilemma, how to write nature without representing nature, the latter a kind of extractivist gesture, and so me conveying this to Bill Burroughs and Gertrude and Alice, who had inquired about my poetry, the kind of stuff I was writing, as if I had to explain such stuff to them. So I knew who Henry David was referring to when he spoke about Bill Burroughs with his two female friends. As it happens, the two women knew Henry David's mother and her wife, as well as his aunt (a hetero, if that matters).

This led naturally to the observation about Eugene being a small world: it's a small world or it's a small town and that's what I love about Eugene, after all, is that sooner or later everybody comes full circle, more or less, though that's *problematic* when you want to be alone, to go to a bar with book in hand and have a good read, scratching stuff in your notebook and having a good think and all, fueled by the elixir of a delicious beer, secure in knowing no one will see you or interrupt you, the kind of security you only really find in big cities like New York, London, and Berlin (those the big cities I used to live in, which is why I mention those ones in particular, even though, I have also lived in Madrid, Addis Ababa, and Belo Horizonte), that sort of situation becoming increasingly impossible now for me in a town like Eugene where everybody comes full circle, such that it becomes increasingly difficult, if not entirely impossible, to get a good read in without getting interrupted by a friend or simply an acquaintance who figures you're really just lonely, being there with book in hand, and so just trying to get attention, what with the book in hand and all, a claim made by my friend Jack

Spicer, in fact, him saying it on more than one occasion—*You know what they say about people who read in bars?*—Spicer enjoying saying this on more than one occasion, always with his little devilish grin, knowing and enjoying the fact that it annoys the heck out of me, such that when I sense he's about to say it again, I nip it in the bud, saying, *Yeah, well fuck that, that's not me*, Spicer getting in his little chuckle over that. We both enjoy annoying each other from time to time, which is the privilege of a good friendship, kind of like marriage, where the whole point of having a spouse is to have someone to dump on when you need to, someone there dear to the heart to tear apart, that's what love's all about, letting it all out, our many warts on full display, tearing into each other or bitching about close friends and how fucked up the world is and so forth. Anyhow, I had been going on about fiction with Henry David, talking about Robert Altman and his film *Short Cuts*, which is based on the short stories of Raymond Carver, and how all the narratives crisscross each other, their separate lives overlapping and so forth. We were at the Highlands drinking Boneyard IPA, the latest hot

IPA, though no one cares about it or talks about it now, this line having been written much later than the first part of the sentence. So when Henry David told me the story about Bill Burroughs etcetera I thought, yes exactly like that, the kind of fiction where there's all these characters who overlap, but in *Short Cuts* they're all oblivious to each other, the setting being LA, after all, until their paths cross in some unpredictable way that forces them each upon the other, whether they like it or not, even though they were there all along, whereas with *Noch Ein* all the characters more or less know each other, Eugene being a small town, essentially, not to say we always like each other or not, that we're happy to see each other all the time, sometimes, for example, not happy at all to see each other, seeing, for example, Spicer coming towards me with his devilish grin and getting annoyed about it already, just thinking about it and getting annoyed, the pleasures of a good friendship. In *Short Cuts*, on the other hand, we, the audience, with our omniscient narrative perspective, see how all the characters have been connected together all along, even though they themselves don't know it. Maxim: *We cross each other but we don't see each other until one day we meet, in some manner or another, yet we're all there together all along, like it or not*

It was last year at this time that Wally suddenly died. I was told that he had cancer, not that he told any of us at the Stein. I had just seen him, had just conversed with him, an old hippie, still dressed that way, with the graying ponytail and the scruffy beard, or was it a goatee, scruffy nonetheless. Seated at the bar next to me, talking poetry, his father having known Kenneth Rexroth, or is that Allen Ginsberg's story? Me surprised one day to hear that Wally had attended a reading by Lew Welch, the "lost poet of the Beat Generation," back in the late sixties. Lew Welch being the poet who came up with the slogan "Raid kills bugs dead," which in the USA is cause for immortalization above and beyond poetry, which may as well be forgotten if even read. Is that why Lew Welch walked off into the forest with a gun never to be seen again, haunted as he was by that *kills bugs dead* line, that that's what he'd be remembered for, not his actual poetry? The only other patron of the Stein who can talk poetry being Allen Ginsberg, except that the said Allen Ginsberg's discussion of poetry usually is limited to the Beats and to his own songwriting, unlike the real AG, the OG-AG, if you will, though I think Allen Ginsberg is basically familiar with the real AG's reading list inside out, Whitman and Blake and all, WCW and all maybe, the said Allen Ginsberg being a folk singer-songwriter of many a clever lyric/song and a highly-skilled classical guitarist to boot, also quite well educated and well-read as well, Eugene being a Beatnik kind of town what with our very own merry prankster, *the* merry prankster himself Ken Kesey—was he a Beat, though? Wally, a large, lumbering bear of a man who brings to mind Charles Olson, who'd I'd call Charlie Olson if I wasn't already calling Jim that, Wally was one of the old hippies who had had his hand in a good portion of Eugene's hippy past and present, including the Country Fair, being like one of the founders of the Country Fair, never mind what it's become today, a kind of neoliberal type Country Fair, everything fucked now by capitalism, as it was then, too, of course, only ramped up more now, with no exit, no end to this end of history

Ran into Jerry and Randi and her man what's his name at the Beck concert last night in Bend. Saw Jerry skirting between the bodies in the crowd ahead of us, caught a glimpse of him but wasn't sure it was him until I saw the back of his jacket with the Stein stuff on it and his arm in a sling. Jerry had recently broken his collarbone in a drunken driving bicycle accident. After he dragged himself off the pavement and after, presumably, realizing his injury, whatever it might have seemed to him at the time, he, in his drunken stupor, hobbled off to his house, still a good distance away, but instead of having one of his roommates take him to the emergency room, Jerry decided to wait until the morning and go to sleep instead, figuring, I guess, that he might just feel better in the morning, or that the throbbing pain in his shoulder, blunted by the alcohol, would like just go away, that it was just a dream he'd had in his drunken stupor, him hoping that at the time. As it happens, he woke the next morning in excruciating pain, unable to move from his bed. So that story's been a big one around the Stein, people, myself included, taking great pleasure and amusement in telling it, this story now coming via the Neo-Stein, that is to say, the Neoliberal Stein (hence the schadenfreude), and how his injury has thrown the kitchen staff for a loop, though that part's serious, I guess, having to account for his month and half or so of absence, staffing being so tight, I gather. Also saw the poet Jim Morrison there in the crowd, with his white patch of hair like an island on the side of his head. He just looked like a body in the crowd, like we all did, in front of the talent on the stage. Beck's intentionally inept eighties guitar solo during one of his songs was one of the many highlights of the evening. Him pretending to rock out like a rock star but not having the licks, this being the kind of poetics I myself am attuned to and have tried to practice in *Noch Ein at the Stein*. It was great running into the Eugene crowd there, and particularly the Stein crowd, which in my opinion may as well be Eugene. When I had pointed out Jerry to Sedgwick, having told the story above to Sedgwick and Henry David the other night when we were on the back porch at the Institute of Loafing sipping cocktails and beers, mine Caldera IPA and Henry David's Fishtail, beers no one pays mention to anymore.

Sedgwick was sucking on a Margarita or a Bloody Mary. One of those perfect Oregon evenings out on the backyard deck, under the Douglas firs (a messy tree), engulfed in green, birds about, owning the place, Stellar's jays and their nest of ninnies, squirrels and such abounding. Spring. Almost summer for real. Not just one of these teasers here and there and then the return of damp, rainy, cold winter, but practically really summer. The winters are not severe here, to say the least. But the damp cold does hit you in the bones, something only a good hot shower or bath can truly shake out. I was thinking this morning how Sedgwick might have concluded from her seeing Jerry, my pointing him out when he was walking up the aisle at the concert, presumably to fetch a beer, looking happy, carefree in his scrappy Eugenian way, though he's from Virginia, "back East," as they say here, even when one is referring to Buffalo, New York, for example, how Sedgwick might conclude that all my friends at the Stein are young like him, like I'm hanging out with all these youngsters, as if I was trying to be young, trying to act like I'm still young. While that may be partially true, in fact I have friends of all ages at the Stein, some like Jack Kerouac, one of the four Jacks, is my age, both of us graduating from the class of 76. Others, like Bill Burroughs, are quite old, Bill Burroughs just turning 83, for example, though, admittedly, there aren't many who are Bill Burroughs's age at the Stein, even if there are plenty of Steinians in their seventies, thank goodness. We often forget about Bill Burroughs's age when we're together at the bar talking at the Stein. But it's hard not to think about it sometimes simply because Bill Burroughs is getting old and his body shows it and also because we are sometimes concerned over Bill Burroughs's health, thinking of some of the Steinians who have passed away recently, like Wally, dying on us around this time a year ago or two, dying out of nowhere, knocking us off guard, the loss of him, no longer there on his stool. And then there are some who are in their forties and some in their sixties and some in their thirties and yes some in their twenties. All this makes me realize that at the Stein, and perhaps in Eugene in general, there's not this strict divide between the generations like there is in so much of the USA, in like Fort Collins, Colorado, for example, except for The Forge Publick House and, okay, a couple others like the Tap and Handle, and, of course, the Town Pump, this qualification coming from my recent experience in Fort Collins as opposed to my previous experiences there. In England the different generations mix, as friends and acquaintances, thanks to the pubs and pub way of life that is so central to English culture, Irish and Scottish and Welsh too, of course. Then I thought that perhaps it was due to weed, and the fact that Eugene is a big weed town, where citizens across the generational divides, as they say, smoke weed on a regular basis, such that it has become part of the life and culture of Eugene, a common scent about town, even before it was legalized. Perhaps it's weed that keeps us young in spirit, such that there isn't this nonsense talk about graduating into maturity, into adulthood, which means achieving something, which means ending your days smoking weed, graduating instead to martinis or wine, cognac perhaps, and of course medications, stabilizers as the novelist Richard Ford calls them in *The Sportswriter*. But the fact that many Eugenians reject this paternalistic claptrap is what makes it such a more or less harmonious place (for some) and perhaps it's this that keeps the generations mingling. But it's just as likely, if not more likely, that it's the hops that perform this function, as much as weed, which now is legal but wasn't then, at the time of this writing, but might as well have been. Though, I think it's probably more accurate to say that it's both the weed and the hops that unite the generations. And even if one is not into weed anymore, having given it up, the daily consumption or the weekly consumption of it, due to various reasons, or if one, like Bill Burroughs, simply doesn't smoke it, but who has tried it on more than one occasion throughout his adventurous life, and who may very well try it again, should the occasion arise, those who aren't smoking the weed do not pass judgment on those who do, are not shocked or threatened or spooked by it like some, like those in Indiana, though there's plenty-o-smoking going on there too, in fact, rampant, like Kentucky, where weed's that state's number one crop. It's a special place, in other words, European-like, in that manner, cosmopolitan even, yet provincial, at the same time, speaking of Eugene here, of course, where the barriers between people float away, thanks to the weed, or not, thanks to the hops, or not, thanks to grapes, too, or not, cheese, too, fresh vegetables, all close by, grown locally, in gardens, in the fields, in the forests, thanks to the cider and the spirits and the mushrooms and the truffles and all the peoples, mostly white, mostly the settler class, me included, sadly so to be sure, just saying, critters, all and one and in between one and all, rocks and such too, slow rocks, laid back shrubbery, loafing trees, firs and pines and madrones and alders and oaks and cedars, babbling brooks and sparkling streams and rolling rivers, everything wet and sloppy and bright when the sun spreads wide in the open skies, the rivers and streams and lakes a'sparkling, and, oh yes, the fish the fish the fish

Everyone, of late, is into the HBO series *Game of Thrones*. I'm tempted at first to say that all *the guys* at the Stein are into *Game of Thrones*, but in fact an equal percentage of the women at the Stein, which, true, are outnumbered by the men at the Stein, are into *Game of Thrones*. And I got to thinking why is that? What is it about the Home Box Office series *Game of Thrones* that has so captured the viewing public, those who can afford the subscription, that is? For it is not just the Steinians that are into *Game of Thrones*, it is the society at large, the subscribing public, that is. I posed this question to Liz Taylor, the other day, that its popularity must be symptomatic of some aspect of our culture, of the zeitgeist, as they say in the Deutschland. I told Liz Taylor that I had noticed how black and white the characters are about things in the subscribers only Home Box Office series *Game of Thrones*. How unwavering most of the characters are in HBO's *Game of Thrones*. Like all the would-be kings and queens vying for the crown and how certain they are that they are the ones who are the rightful heirs. How foreign to our own lives this is, I said to Lizzy T. I mean, said I to Lizzy T, I don't know anyone who says they want to be a king or queen. It must be this desire we have for simplicity, for clean cut, uncomplicated notions of right and wrong, and that this desire must come from the utter absence of such simplicity in our everyday lives. Lizzy T, said wow, you really have thought hard about all this. I said, not really, it's just something I can't help but doing, knowing that many probably think of this trait as kind of obnoxious. Can't you just enjoy what you watch? In response, I say, yes, I enjoy it, and then I rip it apart, which I enjoy too. Later, Lizzy T and I, through our dialectic, countered my thesis above by noting the complexity of some of the characters, like the dwarf. That's about as far into the inquiry we get, as something comes along that requires Lizzy T's attention, while I move back to my book. I think I was reading Bohumil Hrabal's *Total Fears*, reading it in the Stein, with an IPA in hand, or *at hand*, in honor of Bohumil Hrabal himself, who placed so much of his writing in the pubs in Prague, Hrabal, however, likely with a pilsner in hand as opposed to my IPA, in hand or close at hand

Talked with Sophie Lauren at Jiffy Market today. It had been awhile since we crossed paths and she seemed particularly eager to talk, claiming later, when I informed her that I had to leave, that she hadn't had a good conversation for a while. We were both in for lunch. She usually has a glass of wine and I a glass of beer, of course. It's after class for me, while she doesn't teach until later in the evening some time. We were seated at neighboring tables, but I decided to move over to hers, since I had to bend around to talk to her at the table I was at, bend my neck. She explained that she prefers the tables at the front and back of the store, rather than those in the middle. I appreciated the quirkiness of her preference, deciding not to ask her to explain it. Just leave it as it is, a little strange and kooky, as my friend Larry the artist in New York would say. Poets are used to people and their little quirks and their general kookiness. I was a little surprised when she admitted to missing our conversations, implying it by what she said above about not having a good conversation in a while. This is in good part due to our similar backgrounds, she growing up in Nigeria and me growing up in Ethiopia. Also, the fact that she's from New York, though before I got to know her and simply noticed her due to my having seen her both at Jiffy Market and at the college and realizing that she was a fellow "instructor," though she's a full-timer and hence a *professor*, while me, I'm just a part-timer, an adjunky, who therefore teaches part-time classes rather than full-time, full-benefit, job-secured classes. For a long time, she never noticed me, even though we'd occasionally cross paths in the office up on campus. I'm not sure exactly how we ended up conversing that day at Jiffy Market, but I think we were both pleased to learn of our similar pasts. There may have been a bit of flirtation going on there but the fact that we're both married and quite open about it, her mentioning her husband and me mentioning my wife, here and there, in the course of our conversations. We ran into each other more during the Winter term than the current Spring term. Anyway, Sophie Lauren was going on about how unambitious people in Eugene are, at least in terms of the arts. Or how people's taste for art around here is so insulated, all mushy and therapeutic, bad tastes in other words. I concurred, complaining about how difficult it is to interest the local poets in my "experimental poetry" reading series, the poets around here all into poetry that packs an affective punch, poem-inducing emotional epiphanies and all, as if that's all that poetry is about. How I can't get them to come unless I invite them to read. I was still smarting over the no-show for the Linda Russo and Allison Cobb reading. Okay, we had two people in the audience, besides ourselves, but they were Allison's sister and her sister's daughter, and this before there were tons of reading series in town like there is today, each reading series like the other, featuring the same crew of local poets with a splash of outsiders who, nevertheless, all write the same way, that is to say, variations on neo-Romantic, workshop poetry

Went to the Jackalope (or the Lope, as some regulars call it, preferring not to waste their energy pronouncing the whole word) yesterday. On Tuesdays they have $2.50 drafts for all their beers, and they have a good selection of IPAs, including Boneyard, Ninkasi, and Hub, and Hop Valley's Alphadelic (this before the latter brewery went neoliberal, that being planned from the start, apparently). Immediately ran into a former student of mine from a couple years ago. She was more than pleased to see me, sitting there alone at the bar, two glasses full of beverages and a tall can of some crappy beer. She called out to me rather loudly, something like "Oh my god, am I glad to see you. You remember me, right?" I soon discovered that she was drinking a mix of tomato juice and beer and that she was drunk off her ass. She showered me with compliments and asked me to autograph her matchbook. I said, you can't be serious, but then succumbed, wondering what the hell I was doing as I was doing it, *what the fuck*, I thought to myself as I signed her matchbook

She was dressed up for a job interview. Out of work for eight months, she was pretty frustrated and belted out some invectives at the world, loudly for the whole bar to hear. I realized at this point, in part through the bartender's cool response to her, that she had been making a spectacle of herself for quite awhile. What I didn't know was that she was far from over making that spectacle. She'd occasionally remark on how she used to work at the Lope, but when I asked the bartender about it, she shook her head, adding that apparently she worked there for a couple weeks a few years back. Yet here she was going on about it as if she had worked there for years

Bill Burroughs came in around that time and tapped me on the shoulder. Though I didn't dislike her company and in fact enjoyed it to a degree, before, that is, I realized that she was beginning to tip over the edge, I now saw my way out, with Bill Burroughs sitting there waiting for me to join him. I had after all informed her that I was there for the "Safety Meeting," the Tuesday gathering of friends, some, like Bill Burroughs and Jack Kerouac and Charlie Olson, others in the process of becoming friends, bar friends, that is. The Lope, by the way, is adjacent to Eugene's train station. It's a small station, with an old, nicely built and designed brick building, very much what you want in a train station, with these old-fashion kind of wooden benches, all polished from years of use, and people sitting freely on them, waiting for their connection

Overheard at the Highlands that one of the regulars died today, this morning, a heart attack, apparently, out working in his yard, and he wasn't even that old. I wondered who it was, not knowing the names of most of the regulars at the Highlands. Read the other day in *Art Forum* about the death of one my Milano's friends in Manhattan, Jackie McAllister, a bar friend, to be sure, distinct from what most would call an actual friend, even if Facebook has put an end to friends, as a word, and in reality, to some degree, an artist friend from Scotland, who initially made a name for himself with his LEGO paintings of Scottish Tarter plaids. (This being during what artists Nic Arbatsky and Ann Tortorelli dubbed the "Milano's Period" years later when we met again after decades apart.) It was like I was pleased to see his name in *Art Forum*, even if it was a short piece toward the back of the mag announcing his *passing*, as if it was a kind of personal affirmation, affirming what I always thought would eventually be the case, that some of the artists I hung out with at Milano's—my Stein when I lived in *The City*—would eventually become famous—Rirkrit Tiravanija being the most famous of them all, already on his way to fame there at the time with his 303 Gallery show, which amounted to Rirkrit serving up, in the gallery's office, Thai curry to the gallery goers, curry, wine or beer, and, above all, conversation, the sociality of the opening itself being the whole point, never mind the absence of art, that is, an art object or commodity, something to invest in, just how the objects, the object, in this case, being curry, something to eat, brings people together, just like beer brings people together, gets the talk rolling. Rirkrit's subsequent fame, however, was preceded by legendary printmaker Joe Wilfer, Master Printer (and Conversationalist Extraordinaire) at the Pace Gallery, often perched there at the end of the bar, Joe buying me a beer on my first visit to Milano's, enlisting me for life. An affirmation of that and also, of course, of my having been a part of that community, a support-staffer, so to speak, yet, at the same time realizing how pathetic it was to be thinking that way, speaking here of the news of Jackie McAllister's obit, perverse in that it was like I was more concerned about that affirmation/affiliation than his expiration, my piggy-backing off his LEGO paintings instead, they having made a name for himself, though, to be sure, a back-of-*Art Forum* kind of name. True, I said to myself, in self-defense—as if I had to defend myself from my own thoughts—that I actually did also in fact think about his actual dying, wondering how he died, given that he must have been only in his fifties, my thinking the same thing when news of Joe's death arrived in the late 90s, an end to an era

Ran into Janet at Safeway. She seems depressed. Stuck in her job, with nowhere to go. She's now basically stuck with doing her boss's job, but without the equivalent pay. Instead, she's given more hours, but at the same pay as before, this being what her boss called a promotion. We discussed various things, including my utopian vision of a society freed from labor as the dominant action in our lives (my favorite topic) and we both agreed it'd never happen in our lifetimes, at least here, she added. We chuckled at our cynicism as we departed, although, what I didn't tell her was that I actually live my life as if we're already living that utopia, teaching as I do only part-time, my utopia funded by the enslaved Sedgwick with her ten-to-twelve hour corporate shit-hole job, so she in hell and me in heaven, so to speak, what would turn out to be a neoliberal heaven, my heaven based on the invisible economy of her exploited labor, an externality, and so no heaven at'll

Then I turn the corner into the ice cream aisle, an indulgence, yes, but it's on credit, so why not pile on the debt, and run into a former student of mine who has been working for Safeway a number of months now. I asked him how things are going and he said, *Oh, fine, you know, living the American Dream.* We discuss the various things, noting the irony of where we were having our discussion, ironic because my class had focused in part on consumerism

I saw someone, an older man, probably in his late fifties or early sixties, driving by in his new Mercedes Benz sports car and wondered how people can display such signs of wealth without being embarrassed, as if it was natural—*I mean, why live in America* if you can't show off your wealth, celebrate your suckcess*

I had known Charlie Olson at the old Stein, but it wasn't until we moved to the Neo-Stein that Charlie Olson and I became good friends, meaning good enough friends to begin to get together outside of the Stein, whether at the Lope or at each other's homes or wherever. So I was talking to him about losing those two classes that I was counting on and how, though I was subsequently screwed for the summer, the last paycheck coming in mid-July and then that's it until late October, that though I was screwed financially because I was planning on having that income and that I had not saved up for the summer as a consequence, not that I could do so on my paycheck, though I might have been a bit more careful had I known of the upcoming drought, that although I was out of work for the summer I nonetheless felt relieved not to be teaching, to have this time off, thinking it will give me time to get some writing in, maybe return to *Noch Ein at the Stein*, having not written it since the Stein moved house, that is, having not written *Noch Ein* for an entire year and how, as a consequence, I've lost the momentum, that the Neo-Stein had taken the air out of *Noch Ein at the Stein.* "Well, why don't you just publish *Noch Ein at the Stein* as it currently is?" Charlie Olson queried. "But it's not complete," I said. "It's like *Noch Ein at the Stein* was just getting going, finding its stride, when the Stein suddenly morphed into the Neo-Stein, becoming at first a kind of town hall," I said, "but now just another neoliberal establishment designed to generate cash and a quick retirement on the part of its owner-class." "Well, why don't you write about that? Not that I wouldn't do the same if I were in their shoes," said Charlie Olson. "I know, I know," I said, "and I too would likely do the same if someone offered me the cash, being as I am conditioned to think that way, but why not expect more from people, from us? I mean, this is Eugene, hippytown USA. What happened to that hippy spirit?" I asked rhetorically. "I mean, Eugene was one of the cultural capitals of the hippy movement and so also the anti-war movement, the feminist movement, the eco movement, even the civil rights movement, though, not so much the latter as Eugene is basically thoroughly white even if it supported the civil rights movement, the sexual revolution, including gay rights, of course, the overall get high and drop out movement—it was the culture constructed by this movement that put Eugene on the map, helped along by one of its native sons, Ken Kesey, that made Eugene what it is today, at least in name, and then the neoliberals just come along and scoop it up, never having to pay for the cultural capital, to put it in capitalist terms, the cultural *value* constructed by the hippies and their ilk, swooping down with their capital and taking it, as if they had produced it themselves all along, even though, at the time, they did everything they could to quash it, to stop it dead in its tracks

At a certain point in time the Neo-Stein became, like the original Stein, an obsession, more than just a habit, such that the experience soured at times, my sense of becoming a fixture, a kind of joke among the other jokes that had by then become fixtures too. Unlike me, some of the crew from the old Stein managed not to become fixtures, dispersing to the likes of the Lope, for example, though usually at least once a week, they did manage to occasion the Neo-Stein. Jack Kerouac was that way, at least for a stretch, especially early on in the making of the Neo-Stein, the new location being glorious and all, what with its *bells & whistles*, a large digital beer menu board, for example, full of data and such, but also way too large and hence suddenly a larger, seemingly public thing which we had to share now with the rest of the city, some of them not being of Steinian stock at all, changing the make up of the place, or what it had formerly been, which felt like a crowding out of the original Steinians, such that we the original Steinians no longer felt the special sense that a place can imprint on a person, that special sense of belonging to a specific place, with specific company, and the conversation that came from that specific company, kicked up by that specific place. At one point, the management catching onto this feeling among the old Steinians, ordered the bar staff to make a special effort to acknowledge the old timers, the old, original Steinians, some of us older and some of us younger, such that suddenly one of the staff would come by and pat us on the back and act all friendly, maybe hug one of us a little or something. This would seem natural when it came from a Debbie Harry or Lester Bowie, who by the way was a champion hugger, though he mostly confined his hugging to women, women stopping by specifically with a hug in mind, a quick but hearty hug and then bye-bye, though true, men hug on him too, but when one of the new young women would do it, hug us, that is, or one of the new guys behind the bar would try to strike up a conversation, it felt weird, strained, like what the hell we don't really know each other, no need to act like we do. Nonetheless, I and some of the other Steinians did in fact appreciate their gestures knowing that in most cases it was earnest, even when strained, and that we appreciated the management, the owners Burton and Taylor, acknowledging that there was a problem with the Neo-Stein, that you can't just move house and expect things to remain more or less the same in terms of the spirit of the place, and that they may just lose even more of the spirit of the Stein, our so-called cultural capital, if we, the old Steinians, stopped coming to the Stein due to getting lost in the crowd, though, even if we did, did stop coming, going elsewhere, elsewhere instead, it wouldn't matter a whit, insofar as the Stein was doing quite well, thank you, with or without us. In other words, the Stein no longer needed us and our so-called cultural capital, when it really came down to it, but owners Burton and Taylor did in fact seem to care for us, as evidenced by their new policy addressing our seeming alienation, which I at least appreciated, not that we expected special treatment, entitlement and so forth, as if that's bad

It didn't help that the Neo-Stein was just down the street from Reba's ballet. It just made sense to park the car at ballet and saunter over to the Neo-Stein. I would always plan on leaving around 6:30—over an hour before Reba would be finished with ballet—planning on leaving and going home and getting dinner started and then returning to pick up Reba, but my plans almost always got dashed thanks to one of the Steinians coming in, sitting down next to me and hence initiating a conversation and thus forcing me to stay there. Sometimes I'd run into Charlie Olson and then, just as Charlie Olson was leaving, in would walk Bill Burroughs or Jack Kerouac and so I'd agree to have one last "wee one," and so, invariably, those dinner plans would get dashed, this becoming the trend such that it would, admittedly, create problems at home sometimes, some of it exacerbated by Segwick's coming home at irregular hours, though usually late, past eight or so, but sometimes also too early. Banking on the former, which was more the norm, I'd often only get started making dinner at around eight or so and then not have dinner ready for an hour or two after she arrived home. I eventually began to plan better and also sometimes managed to discipline myself better to actually leave early as planned, even when a figure of such interest as Henry Miller would pull up a stool, sneaking up behind me, say, or spotting me across the bar. Henry Miller, a class act with a classy hat or two, was always good conversation and he recognized that in me, I gather. In his early to mid seventies, he, like a number of my older friends, was always good conversation and hence good company, being a class act, in this case. It's not only that Henry Miller was well read and of philosophical mind, it's that he was a good talker, a consequence, in my mind, I came more and more to realize, of his generation, the sixties generation, that is, a period of time I happen to share, though only by virtue of getting in on the tail end of it, my being part of the seventies generation, instead, the sixties dribbling over into the seventies, just before time changed inexorably, thanks to Ronald Reagan and those who followed along with the Ronald Reagan thing, becoming Ronald Reagan in effect. It's not that there wasn't always a Reagan in Americans* all along, it's just that Reagan brought the Reagan out in Americans* (i.e. the worst) and, moreover, that we've been living under the dictates of Reaganized Americans* ever since—even liberals have become Reaganized—dominating everything, setting the agenda for everyone, and so destroying America* for everyone, not that America* hadn't totally destroyed many Americans long before that turn to Reaganism and the so-called *Southern Strategy*. Having attended college in the late 70s and early eighties, I was fortunate enough to have had a taste of the culture that preceded the Reagan decline, a period of time when Reagan was laughed down off the stage of the American* theater, after the Americans* got a whiff of Reaganism in California, of what the Reagan was all about, which, unbeknownst to us at that time, was soon to become what America* would be all about, right up to this very day, seemingly forever, as it turns out. Not to say that plenty of good things, good culture, good poetry, for example, and good beer, of course, for example, didn't slip through the Reaganization grid but all along under the reversals of the Reagan reactionaries, a period of time when each good thing was fought against tirelessly and so forth, right up to this very day, the devastation still going on as we speak

Since leaving the old Stein for the new, Lester Bowie has stumbled some, according to some, though not me, when it comes to service, though this is true of everyone at the Neo-Stein, customer and laborer alike, due to the compound growth of the customer base and the structural layout of the Neo-Stein, all the service directed at the front of the bar where the consumers must line up, the Neo-Stein opting for the DIY approach rather than employing waiters, hence keeping the cost of labor down and thereby optimizing profit, a trend not in any way confined to the Neo-Stein, to be sure. But due to the Neo-Stein's town-hall-like size, which is huge in comparison to the old Stein, which was small, not to mention somewhat ragged, structurally, Lester Bowie's service as a bartender has suffered some, according to some, but not me, since, with all the bartenders at the front of the bar, where the real cash is, leaving only one or, at best two, bartenders to cover the rest of the bar, where the seated Steinians sit. At the old Stein, the diminutive size of the bar enabled Lester Bowie to employ his charm at the same time as performing his labor as a bartender, since there was always one or two bartenders, many charming themselves, there side-by-side beside him, everything wonderfully cramped, on their side of the bar as well our side of the bar, sitting, standing, talking, laughing, and of course drinking, squeezed together cramped-style. Bodies brushing, knocking, hand on shoulder, on waist, back, brushings. Now, due to the large size of the bar at the Neo-Stein, Lester Bowie, at times and sometimes infrequently, cannot help but miss the requests of his customers, they the customers trying to flag down him the worker, the Neo-Stein having turned its patrons into *cunsomers* (customers + consumers = *cunsomers*), due to its large size and its structural make-up, designed to maximize the selling of product. Yet, it is this very design that has resulted in Lester Bowie's diminished efficacy as a *laborer* at the Neo-Stein, in the eyes of some, not me, producing in the former Steinians this revolt against our status as mere *regulars*, each of us now just another *cunsomer* trying not only to get another draft out of Lester Bowie but his undivided, if brief, attention, as well, thereby preventing Lester Bowie from attending to the needs of the other *cunsomers* on the other side of the bar, many of them discovering Lester Bowie's profuse charm for the first time, and so wanting him to linger some, to pause for a story or two or some kind of random exchange, some sort of naughtiness or delightful deviousness or perhaps some little nugget of wisdom or insanity, full of the charm that we all now long for, the charm that comes with engaging Lester Bowie, such charm, by the way, dependent not only on Lester Bowie himself but on Lester Bowie's engagement with others, with us, his interlocutors, all of us coming together like a stylus meeting its groove: out flows the music. Can one be charming alone? No. Even folks like Fred and Ginger perk up when around Lester Bowie, filled with a collective charm, otherwise absented of them, though true Fred and Ginger are often quite perky, perkiness being what they bring to the mix, a kind of nerdy charm, not that Fred doesn't have his dark side. We like their difference (perkiness), however annoying (at times), a result, perhaps, of their being coupled, a perky couple who are nearly always coupled together, the one always there with the other and the other always there with the one. And, since in many ways the Stein's success was due to Lester Bowie's profuse charm (cultural capital), though he was by no means alone in creating this Steinian charm, for example, some saying Debbie Harry was the primary source of such *cultural capital*, Bill Burroughs, for example, particularly drawn in by not only Debbie Harry's considerable charm, but also her down-home looks, down-home but sexy too and warm at the same time, genuinely affectionate, yet not unaware of the spell she casts on dirty old men and dirty young men alike, not to mention the dirty women, and therefore, getting back to what I was saying, because of the success of the Neo-Stein, with its exploding customer base, the word spreading like a virus around town, because of that increase in traffic, Lester Bowie's at times faltering service as a laborer, in my mind, is not only excused but in some ways *necessary*. Necessary because it is this charm that keeps the old Steinians coming back, time and time again, despite the differences between the old Stein and the Neo-Stein, desperate in our attempt to de-transform our status as *cunsomers*, to become Steinians again or, if you will, born-again Steinians, however impossible that now may seem. But, because the bar at the Neo-Stein is so large now, Lester Bowie oftentimes, like all the others, to be sure, cannot see, or chooses not to see, the customers waiting there for a fill or refill, us waiting there in our thirst, in our wanting, as *cunsomers* or not, not only for the next brew on the menu, the next flavor, but also for some of Lester Bowie's profuse cultural capital (charm), however fleeting, due to the many others now, the new customers (total strangers), who having now been subject to Lester Bowie's considerable charm, and hence having increased the demand for said charm, upped the price, wanting more of it, naturally, not that LB cashed in on that demand, price-wise, the tips being distributed evenly amongst all, those with charm and those vacant charm, the tips being shared, not the profits, which is why Lester Bowie eventually cut and run, his charm diluted, not to mention stealthily siphoned off by a member of the upper-management, we were to learn later

At the Neo-Stein, during one of the rare occasions when he was available for conversation, Lester Bowie told me that when Neal Cassidy used to work as a coner for the Forestry Department, or was it some local timber company, his job was to climb up trees and shake the cones down in order to harvest seeds, which is when he came up with the idea of streamlining the job. Instead of climbing up and then climbing down each individual tree (Douglas fir mostly), he climbed up the first tree with the idea of jumping from tree to tree. When at the top of the tree, using the flexibility of the top of the tree to sway back and forth, he could basically step right over to the next tree instead of climbing back down and starting all over again. In this way, he increased his pay exponentially and the productivity of his employer, though, afterwards, I got to thinking of the pressure on the rest of the coners, as a result of his shenanigans, his productivist mindset running roughshod over his fellow coners, who now felt pressured to follow in his step, to maximize productivity by swinging between trees

So I had another one of these episodes where some right wing nut guy goes off on me because of my commie talk, even though it was mild, watered-down socialist basically New Deal talk, at best, he spitting his viper-red face at me like he's going to whip out some weapon and take me out. Bill Burroughs was sitting next of me, to my left, and to the left of Bill Burroughs was the right wing freak who overheard the mildly liberal, quasi-socialist spiel I was dishing out to the Bill Burroughs, making some remarks about its being the first day of Obamacare, so-called, and also the first day of the Republicans shutting down government thanks to that Ted Cruz fucker, the senator from Texas, who, earlier in the week was reciting Dr. Seuss's *Green Eggs and Ham* in protest of the Affordable Care Act, even though the moral of the story is not to knock something until you've tried it, the ACA having just gone into effect. That clearly was over the Ted Cruz's head, even though we're told that the guy has a brilliant mind, that he's super smart, that he knows the law inside and out, which just goes to show you how wrong the super-smart can be, though, I have to question whether such a stupid fuck as the Texan Ted Cruz team can in fact be said to be super-smart at all, because if you use your super-smartness to do stupid things aren't you just a dumb fuck, in the end? Burroughs and I were going back and forth, analyzing the situation, when the wrong-winger guy takes a seat next to Burroughs. I soon had the sense that the wrong-wing nut jobber guy was listening in on our discussion and so I purposely refrained from making any incendiary generalizations about the right wing lunacy and their attempt to sabotage the country, to make America great again. I was feeling a little flustered, not to mention liberal, by how intense the guy was, such that I eventually retreated into Blank Frank mode. Not allowing myself to get all flustered, red in cheek though surely I was, I attempted to employ my Blank Frank tactic of talking in a calm, un-flustered, freakishly reasonable voice, but by then Bill Burroughs was well into it with the wrong-winger, even though, on many fronts, Bill Burroughs was something of a right-winger himself, being a former engineer and real estate agent, though, perhaps contaminated somewhat by my commie talk, I liked to believe, such that due to the wrong-winger's fanatic presence, his butting into and taking over our conversation, Bill Burroughs suddenly found himself talking like a socialist of sorts, defending the ACA (same thing as Obamacare, btw) and all, even though what the wrong-winger clearly wanted to do was to get in *my* face, which he did by accusing me of being a socialist, to which I responded with a shrug, as if to say, okay, yes, so I'm a socialist, so what, at which point the wrong-winger pulled out the old retort about leaving America* if I don't like it, to which I responded, well, this is a democracy and so why should *I* leave, why don't *you* leave if you don't like me exercising my First Amendment rights and so forth, the point is to change things etc and so forth, maybe he should leave himself, I tell him again, in my freakishly calm Blank Frank voice-over, which he eventually did, leaving the Stein, that is, all flustered and self-righteous. Geesh, I said to Bill Burroughs, can't a guy talk about a little socialism here and there without getting etc. Later, I wondered whether the guy had a fire-arm, as they say, whether he was packing heat, imagining a scenario where the guy, frothing at the mouth like some kind of rabid wrong-winger, comes back looking for me and proceeds to shoot up the place, all because of our embrace of the stupid ACA, which is, after all, a Republican policy that keeps the health insurance industry in tact, at the taxpayers expense, milking bodies for everything they've got, etcetera

Ran into George Harrison a couple of days ago at the Neo-Stein. I hadn't seen him in quite a while. He's in town due to some commotion in his marriage. This is common fare for most of us men at the bar who are married. As for those whose marriages don't feel strained (marriage and strained going hand in hand), I figure that's because they're there with their wives, as *couples*, their wives enjoying beer as much as them, hanging out together, as a unit, the two there coupled together, and so seeming to be more or less happy in their marriage, it seems, though I suspect otherwise, that, marriage and strained being part and parcel of marriage itself, they too experience the strain, figuring if they aren't strained then what kind of marriage is that, what sort of collective delusion are they engaged in, being all happy all the time? Am I envious, thought I to myself, in not having such a beer partner? As if you don't want to be alone in your marriage, I said to myself, but also alone and together too, right? Besides, according to a recent article in the *New York Times*, it's better for the marriage, to be loners, loners at times. I remember *George Harrison*'s wife in that HBO documentary saying in response to the question regarding the longevity of their marriage—*How did you make it work? What was your secret?* She saying: "Well, we didn't get divorced." But back now to *my* George Harrison, not the italicized Beatle above. He was feeling depressed and in fact a bit jittery about it. His jitters, though exacerbated by anxiety, a result of a stomach ailment that almost killed him, he tells me. His wife having kicked him out of the house, thus agitating his said stomach condition even more, when in fact it was she who was caught with her hands in the cookie jar, pants down, so to speak, that is to say, in the next door neighbor's bedroom, on his bed, in her underwear and her silk night-shirt unbuttoned so that in effect her boobs were like out there, which, for me, on the other hand, seemed like quite the comical scene, not to mention erotic, even if it was a seeming betrayal. Months later I ran into them at Market of Choice, the overpriced supermarket that pipes in Vivaldi for upscale Neo-Steinian *cunsomers* like me, and so I concluded that they had worked things out. But on that day at the Neo-Stein, George Harrison told me about how, back in the day, he was playing with his band at the Country Fair and how afterwards Ken Kesey came up to him and told him how awesome they were and then handed him and his band some LSD. We both talked about how we had stopped taking psychotropic drugs long ago, more or less, after we had basically gotten what we needed from them, what we had to learn from them, it being all about enlightenment at the time, or so we told ourselves then, before Ronald Reagan came along and banned enlightenment with Nancy's so-called War on Drugs, enlightenment having, as a consequence, disappeared from American* life altogether, thanks to the wrong-wingers who have destroyed America*

We were talking about the space where the old Stein used to be, now called The Cuckoo's Nest, and Corso said something about the changes made to the kitchen and I said something about how sterile the place feels now and then Jerry Garcia told us how he had stepped momentarily into *The Nest*, as it was also referred to, but had to leave right away. I asked Jerry Garcia what he meant by that, whether it brought back bad memories, and he countered, that it was the opposite, that it was a reminder of all that has been lost since the Stein moved to its new location. He said it practically made him sick, nauseated by the realization of what we once had at the old Stein. At first, many at the Stein, including Liz & Dick, said that it was natural to be nostalgic for the old Stein but that the Neo-Stein would eventually become its own place, implying that though it would be something new and distinct from the old Stein, it would become something just as special. And, indeed, due in part to its size, it did become a kind of town hall, with all variety of new *cunsomers* populating its tables and the stools at the bar, a number of whom became good friends. But a full year later, Jerry's reaction to stepping into the old Stein, now called The Cuckoo's Nest, or *The Nest*, made him sick with the realization of what had been lost, implying that the Neo-Stein, with its vastly larger space and with its substantially greater volume of business, had become just that: a business, an engine to generate money. Corso then said something about how much money they are pulling in on a daily basis and so I said my usual thing about it being a shame that there's no profit-sharing policy in place. Corso said that nothing pisses Burton off more than to hear you bring up profit-sharing, that it's just not going to happen, not in the plan. At the old Stein, Dick and Liz were, at least for part of the time, part of the group of friendship that existed between the customers and the employees. While Liz in many ways remains that way, as does Dick for some, the two have faded more into the background, though Liz still manages to engage in conversation, and is in fact quite friendly with me, which I appreciate, I mean, I'm not against the Taylor & Burton team so much as I see their actions, their plan all along to transform the Stein into the Neo-Stein, as being symptomatic of what ails our society at large, everyone out to make a fast buck at the expense of the collective capital that actually goes into making the likes of Taylor & Burton team "successful," regardless of how much time and energy they themselves, admittedly, put into it, that they would be so keen on abandoning the culture they helped give birth to, that they would see that culture simply as the means to enrich themselves alone, rather than sharing the wealth a bit more with their so-called team-members, constructing a future for them too, those whose daily labor and profuse charm helped make the Stein the kind of communist horizon it was, and that so many of their fellow Americans* are exactly like them, whether owners or *cunsomers* or indeed workers, so many of us in this failure of a country so ready and willing to dine and dash, to take the money and run, to so limit our imaginations precisely at the time when it has become so important to imagine a world utterly transformed

I'm totally aware of the fact that I had, all along, been projecting my communist desire for a post-capitalist horizon upon the Stein and the beer community at large with its legion of would-be poets (brewers). Now with the success of the Stein and the success of the beer community at large with its legion of has-been poets (brewers now just the usual capitalists), my projection has been laid bare as the projection it has always been, that the goal, the ten-year plan, had always been, from the very start, to ascend to the ranks of the Neo-Stein, to become the cash cow the Stein was intended all along to be regardless of the various projections on the part of so-called *cunsomers* like me, I'm totally aware of that, but, dear reader, in order to write *Noch Ein at the Stein* it was totally necessary to indulge in this fiction, to imagine the Stein as the creation of something NEW, to imagine the emergence of the beer community at large with its legions of would-be poets as a kind of communist horizon, a post-capitalist grass roots kind of thing that was blossoming before our very eyes, it was necessary, I see now, to project such a horizon onto the likes of the Stein et al in order to give birth to *Noch Ein at the*

Stein, where "communist desire" and "the communist horizon" and " a post-capitalist world" could and do in fact live on, just as it was inevitable, I've come to realize (though not appreciate), that the Stein itself, the real Stein, that is, not my utopian projection of it, would grow into the Neo-Stein, necessary for Liz and Dick in realizing their dream, which, true, had something to do with their family history, but also necessary, in the end, for *Noch Ein at the Stein*, insofar as the Neo-Stein has in the end provided *Noch Ein at the Stein* with a sense of closure, a way to end *Noch Ein at the Stein*, which had, heretofore, no end or ending in sight, nowhere to go to, no narrative arc, no plot, just the immanence of its everyday ramblings about conversations and about pubs being one of the few public spaces left in this neoliberal world, reports from the front lines of a quickly vanishing would-be post-capitalist world where people once gathered for the sheer pleasure of brushing up against friends and acquaintances and strangers, willy-nilly, for no other reason than to seek out their good company, to hear each other's stories, to engage in conversation, and of course, to drink and talk about beer, and so, in that sense, I am grateful for the Stein as well as the Neo-Stein and all those, owners as well as workers, who created the cultural capital out of which the fiction of *Noch Ein at the Stein* has emerged—thanks, guys

It's fitting, then, that a few years after the historically-determined transmogrification of the Stein into the Neo-Stein that I'd run across on Facebook, of all places, news of Bill Burroughs' death. I was shocked to read the sad news, written by Bill Burroughs' daughter, but then I was at the same time not really surprised, given Bill Burroughs' age, now 86 or 87, and that he was beginning to slip some, such that it became harder and harder to make out what Bill Burroughs was saying, my faltering hearing not helping matters any. I felt fortunate, however, that I had had the chance to converse with Bill Burroughs a week before his death, a good death, as it happens, insofar as he died in his sleep, apparently, dying in our sleep being what we're all aiming for, apparently. One of the other Steinians said that he had seen Bill Burroughs just two nights before at the Pint Pot, the new Irish pub just down the street, and that made all of us happy, happy to know that Bill Burroughs had managed to live the life he had wanted to live right up until the end, the life he wanted to live being a life lived in part at the likes of the Stein, a life of drink and conversation and friendship, communist horizon or no, talking about perpetual motion machines and what not, you name it. I then recalled the substance of our final conversation and it reminded me of why I so valued Bill Burroughs' friendship in that Bill Burroughs had always been a friend who I could talk about *anything* with, whether it was my cockamamie meanderings about this and that horizon or whether it was about Bill Burroughs's cockamamie attempt to create a perpetual motion machine, some kind of battery that would self-generate in perpetuity, or his delusional designs on the lovely and ever-popular Debbie Harry

People at the Stein all agreed that Bill Burroughs was fortunate to have died in his sleep and none of us were overly sad about it, having expected it to have happened many times before, even though when it happens it's always a shock, and I, for one, was in fact deeply saddened at the thought that I'd never see Bill Burroughs again, never again have him at my side. I later spoke with Henry Miller, another one of my elder Steinian friends and a purveyor of many a wise nugget, about whether one would prefer to be asleep when one died and whether, when one died in their sleep, one awoke from their sleep, awoke into their death, which I assumed is something like falling asleep, as in falling into death, except you don't wake up, wondering then what it would be like to awaken from sleep into death which is a dream you don't remember. You move from one dream into another dream, the long dream of death, but because there's no sleep involved, just death and the continuum of being dead, there's no dreaming either, but something else, something positively not there. And that, I said to Henry Miller, is where the problem lies with death: you don't get to awaken later to realize what it was like. In that sense, I said to Henry Miller, thinking this through as I went along, we don't actually experience our deaths, experience being something we don't experience at the time of the experience itself but only in hindsight, when looking back on the experience from the hind's eye. People like to say that we'll only know what happens to us after we die *when* we die, but that's only true if there is an afterlife, and one that conforms to our Earthly conception of it, as if the afterlife is basically like being back on Earth, the crucial difference being that one can now *look down* on Earth, somehow, *look down* on what's happening there but also look down on our own past lives, which we now see with the advantage of hindsight, because *that* life is now complete, that is to say finished: *so* <u>that</u> *was my life back there,* <u>that's</u> *what it was, whereas when living it, when "experiencing" it, I didn't know what it was, only that I was in it everyday, but now that it's done I can now see what it was, the life I was living all along.* What we did every step of the way all along every day, now that it's done, makes perfect sense now that it's over, were simply the steps that had to be taken in order for our lives to have been what they were, whereas when we were taking those steps too often we were wondering whether they were the right steps or the wrong steps, not knowing then that there are only right steps, that even the wrong steps are right, even when those wrong steps happen to have been totally wrong at the time, and, for some, totally twisted and damaging at the time, whereas those wrong steps were all along the right steps for you now that you're dead, that is to say complete (i.e. gone), however disastrous if not downright criminal your life may have then in fact have been. It's what you were meant to be, as they say, however devastating that fact is, that that was who you were, who you were all along, disastrous, criminal, or not, now that it's too late to change things, to choose another course. On this last point Henry Miller, the wise elder, disagreed, saying that, while we're still in it, it's never too late to change our lives, to chart another course, within or without being in that course, now as always, and that when we die our life may seem complete, like a narrative with its beginning, middle, and end, when in fact that life keeps going on in the bodies of those we leave behind, if they continue, in their memories and their dreams, the effect our presence and our actions had and still have on others, on those who are still *in it*, and so in that sense, no one is ever complete, ever finished, a kind of happy thought ongoing, or happy ending, even though you're not there to appreciate it, to live it, to see yourself living on in the perishable bodies of others, in the rocks and berries

In our final conversation, I told Bill Burroughs about an erotic dream I had had the night before about one of the female bartenders at the Stein and how it felt like, upon seeing her behind the bar that evening, as if she had experienced this erotic encounter as well. I almost felt compelled to tell her about it but I knew better. That impulse to mention it to her grew out of the visceral sense that she had participated in the encounter and that it wasn't therefore just a dream and that it would thus be rude of me to ignore her, to pretend like nothing happened. In that sense, this impulse to tell her, to discuss the dream with her, was more like the desire to discuss things the next day, after the night of love-making, saying something like "that was nice, last night" or "I really enjoyed our evening together" or "that was really wonderful" or "that was really beautiful last night," not mentioning "love-making" or "fucking," as in "I really enjoyed fucking you last night" or "I really enjoyed your fucking me last night, especially the part where you etcetera" though in my case, my case with her in the dream, it was just making out, just kissing, which can be every bit as erotic as the love-making, the coitus, every bit as erotic as that part where you etcetera. I was feeling kind of guilty just talking about it with Bill Burroughs, her there and all behind the bar, serving and talking with us like we were the friends that we were, and me talking about it with Bill Burroughs right up to the point in which she served us our drinks, and so I told him that, about feeling guilty and kind of weird, and Bill Burroughs brushed it aside as nonsense, that there was nothing wrong with enjoying the dream, the experience, or, for that matter, thinking erotically of the bartenders, in dreams or otherwise, even if we were too old for them, though, he was, to be sure, close to thirty years my senior, and therefore *much too old* for them compared to my being merely simply *too old* for them, not to mention married and so happily whatever. But then that was Bill Burroughs who, though well into his eighties, still fantasized plenty about the bartenders at the Stein, especially, if not famously, the charming and delectable Debbie Harry, who, by the way, all the men, young and old, had a crush on, some even deluded into thinking that there was something actually going on there between them, the old or young man and the ever charming and delectable Debbie Harry, who just one day got up and left, marrying, inexplicably, some military stud back East, much to our collective devastation. Bill Burroughs got away with plenty of hugs from the bartenders at the Stein, thanks to his age, which he totally exploited, and of course his abundant charm. Not that they didn't know what was coursing through Bill Burroughs's mind, what was going on in there, though it wasn't all dirty, much of it genuine affection, ambiguity coursing through it all. It wasn't just that Bill Burroughs was what they call a dirty old man, which he was, of course, it was that Bill Burroughs was also a dirty young man who, at such times, tended to forget he was old, but now that he was in fact old, he could get away with it, being now a dirty old man, yet a polite and charming dirty man, even though when he was a young man he was already thoroughly a dirty old man. Not that women aren't dirty old men, too. As for those bartenders who hugged and sometimes kissed Bill Burroughs on the cheek, I'm not sure what was going on with them, what it was about younger women and old men, why they were so affectionate toward dirty old men like Bill Burroughs, as if they didn't know their effect on Bill Burroughs, as if they didn't know that Bill Burroughs still entertained fantasies of something actually happening, being a dirty young man stuck in a dirty old body. Perhaps, it was that, being young, they didn't quite know yet, in a visceral way, that when you're old you're still young, that age is something that blind-sides you, such that you have to keep reminding yourself that the body others see when looking at you is no longer the young body you knew when you were younger, and that, because they are young, they the waitresses in question, pre-sumably think that being old is like some other life, though of course, come to think, they, being women, are also all too aware of this passing of time and what awaits them, being, as they are, constantly judged, perpetually under scrutiny by old men and young alike, not to mention women, young and old alike, so maybe, come to think, this applies more to young men than young women, the above being more about how I used to think of it, of time and aging, where old age was some other, distant country I would never really have to visit or arrive at anytime soonish, that I had all the time in a world that once had all the time in the world, and that the world of old age, of being a *senior*, was forever out of reach (or gone), would never come to pass, that I would never find myself in an old body, dirty or not, longing for the touch of others, young or old, just another old man, sitting alone at the bar, flirting with the bartenders, a companion to saddle up to, with a beer in hand, waiting for some hugs to come my way

Tim Shaner is author of *Picture X* (Airlie Press 2014) and *I Hate Fiction: A Novel* (Spuyten Duyvil 2018). He received a Ph.D. from SUNY-Buffalo's Poetics Program in 2005. His work has appeared in *Exquisite Pandemic, The Poetic Labor Project, Plumwood Mountain: An Australian Journal of Ecopoetry and Ecopoetics, Capitalism, Nature, Socialism, Colorado Review,* and elsewhere. With Kristen Gallagher he curated the Rust Talks series on poetics in Buffalo and edited *Wig: A Journal of Poetry and Work*, and he published, with Jonathan Skinner, the pamphlet *Farming the Words: Talking with Robert Grenier* (2009).

Made in the USA
Las Vegas, NV
13 April 2022

47418113R00125